C000084507

Imprimatur

The Social Register

Thank You

I want to thank Kathryn Court and Gerry Howard of Viking Penguin for giving me the opportunity to introduce the rich girl to such a wide audience. I also want to thank my agent, Tony Gardner, and Kate Thornton, who patiently typed and retyped the manuscript.

Finally, I am especially indebted to John O'Brien, who encouraged me to share my knowledge of and love for the rich girl with poor boys throughout the country.

PENGUIN BOOKS

THE POOR BOY'S GUIDE TO
MARRYING A RICH GIRL

Mr. Duffy attended private schools in Connecticut. He is a graduate of the University of Virginia and received an M.B.A. from the Harvard Business School. He lives in New York where he works as an investment banker.

The Poor Boy's Guide To Marrying A Rich Girl

Brian Ross Duffy

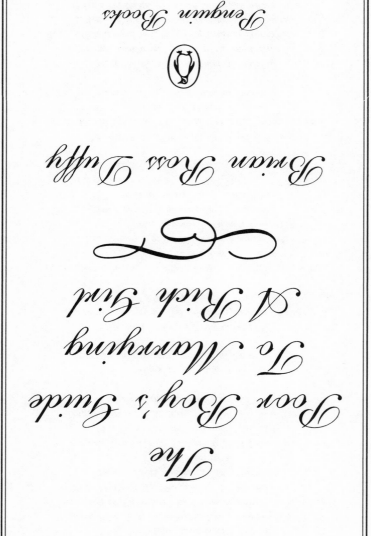

Penguin Books

PENGUIN BOOKS

Viking Penguin Inc., 40 West 23rd Street,
New York, New York 10010, U.S.A.
Penguin Books Ltd, 27 Wrights Lane, London W8 5TZ
(Publishing & Editorial) and Harmondsworth, Middlesex,
England (Distribution & Warehouse)
Penguin Books Australia Ltd, Ringwood,
Victoria, Australia
Penguin Books Canada Limited, 2801 John Street,
Markham, Ontario, Canada L3R 1B4
Penguin Books (N.Z.) Ltd, 182–190 Wairau Road,
Auckland 10, New Zealand

First Published in Penguin Books 1987
Published simultaneously in Canada

Copyright © Brian Ross Duffy, 1987
Illustrations copyright © Viking Penguin, Inc., 1987

LIBRARY OF CONGRESS CATALOGING IN PUBLICATION DATA

Duffy, Brian Ross.
The poor boy's guide to marrying a rich girl.
1. Dating (Social customs)—Anecdotes, facetiae,
satire, etc. 2. Mate selection—Anecdotes,
facetiae, satire, etc. I. Title.
PN6231.D3D84 1987 818'.5402 87-6933
ISBN 0 14 00.9721 X (pbk.)

Printed in the United States of America by
R. R. Donnelley & Sons Company, Harrisonburg, Virginia
Set in Galliard
Designed by Beth Tondreau Design

"RICH GIRLS DON'T MARRY POOR BOYS,
JAY GATSBY."
—Daisy Buchanan,
in *The Great Gatsby*
by F. Scott Fitzgerald

"IT'S JUST AS EASY TO MARRY A RICH GIRL
AS A POOR ONE."
—My father

Preface

$\mathcal{O}$ne of my close friends, who eventually married a young woman of immense wealth (her family's home in Palm Springs was once described as a medieval barony), always referred to his female companions as "candidates." His philosophy, although eminently successful, was much too deliberate (at least for me) and certainly not romantic; after all, marriage is not an election. Of course, he's paid a high price for his success: his life is full of social and financial obligations. He winters in Palm Springs, summers in both La Jolla and Newport (he has his own plane), plays polo with princes and archdukes, and Concordes regularly to Europe. He's no longer a free man. He's a member of the board of museums, ballets, and symphonies, dines with people called Hearst, Rockefeller, and Ford, and appears at endless charity galas and events. He must spend several hours each week consulting with his money managers, tax accountants, and lawyers. By any standard, he's fully employed.

The purpose of this book is to introduce you, the poor boy, to that very special world of the rich girl; for, as F. Scott Fitzgerald so eloquently warned, "the rich are different from you and me." I hope that *The Guide* will narrow those differences and allow you, the poor boy, to put them in their proper perspective. *The Guide* is written to assist you in appreciating the world of the rich girl economically—i.e., with a minimum of time, effort, and expense. It is designed to facilitate your meeting, courting, and marrying the right rich girl. *The Guide* is intended for the serious reader.

Preface

The decision to begin this project was made following a lengthy dinner conversation with a noted economist in Washington, D.C. Although a neoconservative, he has always been suspiciously egalitarian. That evening, he suggested that an upwardly mobile society is characterized by the frequency with which poor boys marry rich girls. He argued strenuously that the marriage of the poor boy and the rich girl created a more stable and more dynamic, productive society. He viewed the union of these unequals as the ultimate and socially most acceptable transfer payment. In subsequent meetings with this economist and his colleagues at the American Enterprise Institute, I was advised that the neoconservative sociologists and economists consider it the social obligation of the poor American boy to marry a rich girl. They called this obligation *noblesse oblige*.

Apparently even Marx appreciated the significance of such a union and had conflicting reactions. On the one hand, he viewed it as a threat to the dialectic, while on the other he viewed it as communism in its purest form. His lengthy correspondence with Engels frequently mentioned such marriages as the "opiate" of the upper-middle class.

Both the left and right, therefore, have viewed the union of the poor boy and the rich girl as a significant social event. Reading *The Guide*, therefore, can be justified no matter what your present political inclinations may be.

While writing *The Guide*, I've been constantly reminded of American novelist John O'Hara's advice that the successful author must write about what he knows best. By both circumstance and background, I've come to know and appreciate the rich girl. I grew up with her, studied with her, summered with her, and dated her. I've dined with her, drunk with her, danced with her, and laughed with her. I've slept with her and wept with her (at her Nanny's funeral). Many rich girls remain my closest friends and confidantes. I know the rich girl very well, and I can only hope that *The Guide* validates O'Hara's advice.

In regard to this book's opening epigraphs, by the way: Daisy

Preface

Buchanan was entirely wrong, and my father was right. Rich girls do marry poor boys—even the Greeks and Romans did it (read your Homer, Plato, and Ovid). The choice, however, is yours. There are thousands of eligible rich girls who are bright, attractive, and loving. Many will make excellent wives, lovers, and Mummies (contrary to current opinion, these categories need not be mutually exclusive). I hope that you will find *The Guide* informative and practical and that your own success in meeting and marrying the right rich girl will be an inspiration for other poor boys to follow.

--------------------- $ ---------------------

Like all authors I'm obliged to thank those individuals, whether friends or acquaintances, who volunteered their assistance and made this book possible.

I am especially grateful to Cornelia Guest, Patty Hearst, Cosima Von Bulow, and Caroline Kennedy, for each was a constant and considerable source of information and inspiration, and without them and other rich girls (too numerous to name) this project would never have been completed. Special thanks to Princess Stephanie of Monaco and her charming sister Princess Caroline. Stefano, you're a very lucky fellow!

I must, of course, acknowledge my colleagues in journalism, especially the editors of *Town & Country, W, Vanity Fair,* and *Palm Beach Life* for their unqualified assistance and encouragement in what proved to be a much easier undertaking than originally anticipated.

I wish every poor boy the best of luck on what I hope will prove to be a profitable and enjoyable adventure.

Palm Beach
December 1986

Contents

Contents

PART THREE: THE COURTSHIP

PART FOUR: THE PROPOSAL AND ENGAGEMENT

APPENDICES

Part One

Introduction and Profile

Chapter One

Clues to the Mystery

*T*he rich girl has remained a mystery for the poor American boy for far, far too long. For many of you it must seem like an eternity. She has been an object of curiosity and comment for centuries and an enigma that only a fortunate few have ever solved. It seems that the more that has been written about her, the more confusion that continues to persist. It's a tragedy of sorts. *The Guide* is designed to end this unfortunate state of confusion once and for all. It will help you meet, court, and marry the right rich girl for you.

As the first step in penetrating this mystery and sharing the wealth of a rich girl's life, I've outlined thirteen clues (a poor boy's dozen) which will aid you in identifying and understanding the rich girl. Although only an introduction, this chapter will assist the poor boy in appreciating how very different the rich girl's world really is. Don't be intimidated, however, for these differences can be bridged quickly and economically. That's what *The Guide* is all about: it is a bridge to a new and better life, a salient to upward mobility.

Since food is central to the rich girl's life, let's begin there.

The Poor Boy's Guide

Clue #1 : Her Food

Rich girls almost never eat breakfast, which they consider boring. They would much rather conserve their limited calories (rich girls budget calories, never money) for a later, presumably more interesting meal (i.e., a dinner which begins with caviar, oysters Rockefeller, or smoked salmon, and ends with *your* chocolate mousse). There is, of course, the notable exception. Rich girls are accustomed to eating breakfast after a benefit, charity ball, debutante party, or gala. This meal is served between midnight and two A.M. in a large hotel or at a private club by waiters who don't speak English. I've always found that the food is poor and frequently cold, but the music (and company) is usually good.

Lunch was initially designed for two rich girls. . . .
It has since become a more universal meal.

Rich girls sometimes eat lunch, especially when they can eat with another rich girl. Lunch was originally designed for two rich girls to discuss last night's dinner party, the upcoming benefit, or the latest designer fashions; lunch has since become a more universal meal. While discussing the party, the benefit, or the most recent designs at lunch, rich girls eat salads (typically shrimp, crab, or lobster), smoked salmon, and imported cheese and fruit. Rich girls never eat bologna or salami; they have never even *heard* of liverwurst. Rich girls, in fact, eschew sandwiches completely. They used to eat quiche for lunch, but that was before everyone else did. Of course, the favorite snack for a rich girl is caviar and a split of champagne. Very, *very* rich girls eat caviar like ice cream—no eggs or onions, just right out of the jar with a spoon.

Rich girls enjoy eating with their hands and fingers and so are partial to finger food (canapés, hors d'oeuvres, and appetizers). They have practiced intently for years at debutante parties, embassy receptions, cocktail parties, and society weddings, and are remarkably adept at "fingering." It's a practice that I've personally come to enjoy.

For dinner, rich girls love expensive food with French or Italian names. Rich girls almost never eat meat, although a few will discreetly nibble on filet mignon or a rack of lamb. Instead, they prefer seafood and shellfish of almost any kind. Rich girls do, however, love dessert—*your* dessert. Rich girls can at times (albeit infrequently) be extremely disciplined and realize that dessert is damaging to their figures, their skin, and their teeth. They, therefore, almost never order dessert for themselves. Instead, they ask *you* to order a dessert (always one which they like) and ask for two spoons. Expect to share all desserts, but please keep the plate on your side of the table.

Some rich girls suffer from serious eating disorders: they can't decide when and how much to eat. Some rich girls can't stop eating at all; they are called *bulimics*. Some rich girls never eat; they are called *anorexics*. Avoid both.

Her Favorite Foods

The rich girl's constant invitations to elegant dinner parties, her late-night excursions to fashionable new restaurants, and her frequent travel abroad have all exposed her to many different types of food. Whether it's ethnic, Oriental, Mexican, Cajun, or the stunning colors and minuscule portions of nouvelle cuisine, the rich girl has tasted it all. There are a few dishes, however, that are the staple elements of her diet. They are the rich girl's favorite foods.

Starters

Caviar
Oysters Rockefeller
Smoked Salmon
Lobster Cocktail
Crab Cocktail
Shrimp Cocktail
Asparagus Vinaigrette
Tomato & Mozzarella
Prosciutto & Melon
Artichoke Royale

Entrees

Caviar
Lobster Thermidor
Crab Imperiale

Soft-shell Crab
Crown of Lamb
Golden Snapper
Silver Salmon

Dessert

Caviar
Strawberries Romanoff
Raspberries
Vanilla Mousse
Chocolate Mousse
Crème Brûlée
Profiteroles
Zabaglione
Any kind of Soufflé

Clues to the Mystery

CLUE #2 : HER RELIGION

All rich girls subconsciously want to be Episcopalians . . . most already are. Rich girls are usually not at all religious and certainly don't want a religion with demanding rules and regulations. Rich girls may be opinionated, but they certainly are not dogmatic. Instead, they want a religion with "social" awareness, attractive churches in the best neighborhoods, comfortable pews, and short services scheduled at reasonable hours. It's no wonder they all pray to be Episcopalians.

In fact, organized religion really doesn't matter to the rich girl. Sure, she's a believer, but for you—the poor Catholic, Protestant, Jewish, or Muslim boy—your religion, or lack thereof, just doesn't seem to matter. She'll make the final judgment on you based on other factors (see Chapter 13, "Your Prospects").

God works in strange ways, doesn't He?

CLUE #3 : HER DRINK

The rich girl's taste in drink is very fluid. The only constant how-ever, is champagne, which remains the rich girl's favorite tonic. Ever since the blind monk Dom Pérignon invented the *méthode champagne,* the rich girl has enjoyed this effervescent wine. A close friend of mine from a distinguished Catholic family claims Dom Pérignon is her patron saint.

Champagne has been the drink of nobility for over three cen-turies and for a very good reason. As Madame Pompadour noted, "Champagne is the only wine that leaves a woman more beautiful after drinking it!" It's certainly a very good excuse. Of course the most famous rich girl of the eighteenth century, Marie Antoinette, consumed a bottle of Moët & Chandon (Brut, 1779) before her death by beheading. She died a very happy queen and left a great deal of furniture for the rich girl's Mummy to purchase and enjoy.

Recommended Champagnes

You must familiarize yourself with champagne, since you will be buying and drinking a great deal of it. You'll be consuming endless magnums and jeroboams while pursuing the rich girl of your choice. Here's a list of some of those champagnes which I consider the very best.

Roederer Cristal
The very best. A soft and mellow approach but a very dry finish. Appropriate for a quiet evening alone.

Dom Pérignon
A classic. An impressive and penetrating slender stream of very fine bubbles. Very, very good in bed.

Perrier-Jouët
Terribly dry and straightforward, although occasionally fruity, nutty, and masculine. Makes a perfect house gift for Mummy.

Taittinger Brut
Fine color and sparkle with a fragrant springlike aroma and flavor. Excellent choice for an outing or polo game.

Moët & Chandon White Star
Engaging and lively but sweet on the nose and palate. Perfect for catalogue reading.

Clues to the Mystery

Bollinger	A very lively and distinctive champagne. Generously effervescent. Highly recommended for benefit committee meetings and charity affairs.
Veuve Clicquot	Very, very fresh and invigorating. My favorite breakfast champagne.

CLUE #4: Her Reading

Rich girls read constantly. They read *Town & Country, Palm Beach Life, W, Women's Wear Daily,* and *Vanity Fair.* Some rich girls even subscribe to foreign publications, which are usually written in French or Italian. These publications are typically very thick and extremely heavy. Some make the Yellow Pages appear light. Even if the rich girl can't read the text, she can devote hours, sometimes even days, to studying the many high-fashion editorial photographs of jewelry, clothes, shoes, accessories, and the hundreds of pages of enticing advertising.

Rich girls never read *Good Housekeeping* (they have or will have their own housekeeper), *Women's Day* (rich girls collect jewelry, not recipes), or *Family Circle* (rich girls have their own circles—they're called swims). Some rich girls do read *Gourmet*—it's often a valuable source of menus for Mummy's chef or the caterer.

Unfortunately, during the summer the quality of a rich girl's reading deteriorates dramatically and suddenly. *The National Enquirer* and *The Star* make their appearance, for they are the perfect reading for Bailey's Beach (*the* beach club in Newport), the country club pool, or Daddy's yacht.

9

The rich girl is very well read.

The favorite reading material for the rich girl, however, remains the catalogue. Rich girls receive more catalogues than any other type of mail (excluding invitations). One of my very best friends, who travels with her catalogues, insists that she receives at least one catalogue daily. She's prone to understatement: her apartment is *littered* with catalogues. It looks like a mailroom.

Finally rich girls love reading books about royalty and other rich girls, especially Barbara Hutton, Gloria Vanderbilt, and Grace Kelly (see Chapter 7, "Legends").

Unfortunately some rich girls can't read at all; they are called dyslexic.

CLUE #5 : HER FIGURE

I've never met a rich girl who isn't thin (Christina Onassis excluded). Even if they weren't born thin, they learn at a very early age to adhere to Babe Paley's admonition that "you can't be too rich or too thin." If absolutely necessary, Mummy may send her little rich girl to a special "reducing" camp during the summer

Clues to the Mystery

break from Foxcroft, Hockaday, or the Bishop's School. Later, before she joins her first swim, she may visit with Mummy special "farms" or "spas" such as Maine Chance, Canyon Ranch, or the Last Hope. These spas, which can cost thousands of dollars to attend, are the rich girl's ultimate solution to calories.

*C*LUE #*6* : *H*ER *P*ETS

Most rich girls are not especially fond of animals, although horses and the occasional dog are the clear exception. The rich girl's hectic social and travel schedule typically precludes having any kind of pet unless someone else can take care of it. This is the principal reason rich girls love horses: a horse is nearly impossible to keep at home or in the apartment. Horses simply don't travel well. Instead, horses are kept in stables where someone else, usually a groom or stable hand, will feed, brush, and exercise them.

Some Freudian psychologists have argued a more subliminal reason for the rich girl's deep emotional attachment to the horse. These theories have included the Godiva Complex and the Catherine Complex. Consult your medical dictionary or ask your own psychiatrist for a more complete explanation.

*C*LUE #*7* : *H*ER *M*EDICINE *C*ABINET

The medicine cabinet contains the sprays, soaps, cosmetics, emollients, and fragrances which are absolutely essential to the rich girl's survival. The rich girl and the poor boy should be forever appreciative of Estée Lauder, Charles Revson, and Elizabeth Arden, all of whom deserve plaudits for historic preservation.

The Environmental Protection Agency has estimated that this proliferation of aerosol sprays will ultimately destroy our ozone level. Despite this warning, a rich girl has "sprays" for every part of her body: hair sprays, arm sprays (deodorants), mouth sprays, vaginal sprays, and foot sprays. She may have more than one kind of each and typically uses them several times a day. A former friend of mine had a specially designed travel case to accommodate up to twelve sprays—it still was never enough. She constantly pleaded with me to carry some of her sprays. For this and other reasons, most rich girls are not environmentalists.

CLUE #8: HER BEST FRIENDS

The rich girl's sunny disposition and Daddy's cottage at Newport or Sea Island, or the ski lodge in Aspen, Vail, or Sun Valley have all contributed to her overwhelming popularity. She's constantly in demand. She has many, many friends, especially other rich girls and society boys. (The society boy is the constant companion of the rich girl, and is devoted to organizing and attending as many social events as is physically possible.)

The diamond and other precious gems, however, are the rich girl's very best friends. Rich girls have been collecting diamonds

The Jewelers

The poor boy will want to learn a great deal about diamonds and the other gems for, with a successful proposal, he'll be buying rings, clips, pendants, broaches, chokers, bracelets, necklaces, and earrings for his very own rich girl. I encourage you to visit many of these major jewelers to get a first-hand impression of the rich girl's very best friend. Remember the romance of diamonds and the right rich girl can be forever.

Van Cleef & Arpels	Tiffany & Co.
Chaumet	J. & E. Caldwell Co.
Cartier	Fred Joaillier
Bulgari	Bailey Banks & Biddle
Harry Winston	Shreve & Co.

and other precious gems for centuries. Rich girls wear diamond, sapphire, ruby, and emerald rings, clips, pendants, brooches, chokers, bracelets, necklaces, and earrings. Very rich girls wear diamond-and-sapphire tiaras; they are called *princesses* (see Chapter 6, "Special Situations"). These gems are often combined with gold, silver, and platinum to create jewelry. One of my best friends insists that collecting jewelry is the rich girl's version of a competitive sport. Of course, many rich girls innocently continue to believe that the jeweler is the world's oldest profession(al).

Clue #9 : Her Circulation

No, it's not a physical system, although it certainly consumes a lot of energy. You will never read about it in textbooks (with the exception of *The Guide*) or in the *Journal of Internal Medicine*. Instead, circulation is simply a way of life for each and every rich girl that I have met. It's typically her principal preoccupation and in some cases seems much more like an *occupation*.

After all, the rich girl is above all a social creature. She has never led a solitary or confined existence and has never been an introvert. Instead, at a very early age the rich girl learns the value of circulating (mixing and socializing). In fact, the rich girl's life is one of endless circulation: She "preps," "comes out," and "swims"—each of which she does with other rich girls (and sometimes boys).

I've always found that, whether it's a barbecue on the ranch in Texas, a charity ball at the Plaza Hotel in New York, a debutante party at the country club, or simply a dinner dance on Mummy and Daddy's estate, the rich girl is always circulating. Circulating, like breathing, comes naturally to the rich girl.

You'll want to find a rich girl who improves your own circulation.

CLUE #10 : HER SECURITY

The rich girl is very conscious of security: not national security or social security, but her *own* security. She's read about kidnappings and ransom notes, and has been constantly reminded by Mummy and Daddy of the very real danger of being rich. She may have lived behind massive gates, in private enclaves with guards and watchdogs, or in co-ops and condominiums with liveried doormen to check her guests. She's almost certainly familiar with peep holes, dead bolts, all kinds of locks and keys, and the latest in electronic security.

Some very rich girls have their own security. These are called guards. I've known several rich girls who travel with, and eat with, and (on occasion) even sleep with their guards. I used to date a rich girl who had her own special kind of security. It was called a detail. Each and every date was a double date. Herself, myself, and her security detail. It was quite an intimidating experience. It was a complicated and very, very guarded affair.

CLUE #11 : HER LANGUAGE

The rich girl has a vocabulary of her very own. These are words, phrases, and expressions peculiar to her very special and at times exclusive world. For many poor boys, the rich girl is simply impossible to understand. If you're to succeed in this venture, you'll want to learn her idioms as quickly as possible and use her vocabulary constantly (see Appendix A, "The Poor Boy's Dictionary").

CLUE #12 : HER QUALITIES

Rich girls constantly display many admirable qualities which are known collectively as "breeding." These qualities are instilled at a very early age by Nanny, by Mummy and Daddy, or by the headmistress (or master) at boarding school. The rich girl is unselfish, kind, considerate, disciplined, tolerant, enthusiastic, cheerful, honest, and loyal. (No, she's not thrifty; she was never a Girl Scout.) For you, it's critical that she be generous and full of trust(s).

She remains ready and willing to contribute her time and money to worthwhile causes; these are called benefits. She is kind and considerate of others and is anxious to assist any friend in need. Although disciplined, she is tolerant of weaknesses in others, especially society boys. She can be a reservoir of enthusiasm and a dependable shower of cheer.

Of course, there are two sides to every coin and to each and every rich girl. She can be selfish, inconsiderate, undisciplined, intolerant, lethargic, and moody. In short, she's probably terribly spoiled.

CLUE #*13* : HER FAVORITE HOBBY

Rich girls do have hobbies—but they don't include collecting stamps or coins. Instead, rich girls collect jewelry, gems, antiques, pictures, and porcelain vilebots and cachepots, among many other objects. Rich girls can be terribly acquisitive.

The favorite hobby of every rich girl, however, is shopping, for her demanding professional and social life and her frequent travel to other climates requires closets full of shoes, clothes, and fashionable accessories. Her considerable social demands compel her to purchase cruise wear, sportswear, evening wear, beach wear, ski wear, lounge wear, and underwear.

Rich girls charge these clothes (often to Mummy and Daddy) in stores called Bergdorf Goodman, Bonwit Teller, I. Magnin, Henri Bendel, Neiman-Marcus, and Montaldo's. For some rich girls shopping becomes more than a hobby—it's closer to a *profession*. One of my best friends confessed that her exacting social schedule demanded a professional commitment to shopping. She works more than nine to five—she's on overtime, she claims.

Some very rich girls will go to great lengths to shop. They travel with Mummy to Paris every year to see the fall and spring collections. Almost twenty fashion houses preview their fashion collections each and every year to rich Mummies and their daughters. The preview is a terribly exciting event with famous designers who have ponytails or large glasses, models on runways, photographers, and all the Mummies and rich girls crowding into gilded grand ballrooms for glimpses of what clothes they should and must buy. It's an extravagant form of shopping. This is called couture. Some rich girls confuse couture with culture. It's so easy to be confused these days.

Favorite Catalogues

The catalogue advertises the necessities of a rich girl's life, including jewelry, perfumes, clothing, accessories, and food, and for that reason it is an integral part of her life. The catalogue is the rich girl's version of a best-seller. The favorite catalogues of the rich girl include the following; they are required reading for any poor boy with a serious interest in the rich girl.

Tiffany & Co.	Silver, china, jewelry
Gucci	Leather, accessories, luggage
Neiman-Marcus	Literally everything
Bergdorf Goodman	Fashions from all over the world
I. Magnin	Designer fashions and much more
Godiva	Chocolates
Loewe	Leather handbags, luggage, and accessories
Pratesi	Sheets and linens
Shreve & Co.	Jewelry and gifts
Pierre Deux	Country French everything
Hammacher Schlemmer	The ultimate in gadgets
Hermes	Perfumes and fine clothing and accessories

Chapter Two
Home Sweet Home

$\mathcal{R}$ich girls traditionally have several homes. They grow up in large houses called mansions, or on estates in suburbs called Greenwich, Grosse Pointe, or Lake Forest, or in co-ops and condominiums on Fifth Avenue, Nob Hill, or Beacon Street. They have large summer homes called cottages, farms in Kentucky or Virginia, ranches in California or Texas, or ski lodges in Aspen, Vail, or Sun Valley. Rich girls have never lived in subdivisions, split-levels, or trailer parks. Rich girls live *on* a ranch, not *in* a ranch.

Some rich families insist on living very, very close together. They purchase or build several large homes on adjacent parcels of land, erect imposing fences or walls, grow towering hedges, and employ private security guards. They then call this a compound. The Kennedy family invented this way of life, among many other things. It's their great contribution to our society.

Rich girls have always lived on hills. Since medieval times, hills have provided safety (castles and citadels were built on hills), the best climate (sunshine and perennial breezes), freedom from disease (sewage runs downhill), and, most important, a marvelous vista from which to view less affluent peers. This custom continues today, whether on Chestnut Hill (Philadelphia), Carnegie Hill (New York), Beverly Hills (Los Angeles), Beacon Hill (Boston), or Mission Hills (Kansas City). "Head for the hills" has a whole new meaning now, doesn't it?

Home is particularly important to the rich girl. First, Mummy and Daddy live at home and the rich girl is particularly attached to her parents. She is their creation, in a more than strictly physical sense. Second, so much has happened at home—the sweet-sixteen party, Mummy's party for the President, the rich girl's coming out, the dinners for Placido, Mikhail, and Liz. Finally, home really sets a rich girl apart: it is full of pictures (paintings), Oriental rugs, family heirlooms, and antiques purchased in London or Paris. The rich girl's home is often like a museum, and sometimes is so spectacular that it's been featured in lengthy articles in *Town & Country, Architectural Digest,* or *House & Garden.*

Behind those hedges and stone walls, or down those long driveways that curve into the distance are châteaux, Tudor mansions,

Rich girls have always lived on hills. . . . Head for the hills has a whole new meaning.

and enormous columned colonials owned by Mummy and Daddy. The rich girl's house has at least a couple of rooms that most other homes simply don't have. Whether designed for social, athletic, religious, or purely practical purposes, these rooms truly distinguish the rich girl's home. There may be a ballroom (for dancing, silly!), a gallery (for paintings), a library (for books and manuscripts), a squash court (for the sport), or a screening room (for Daddy's movies)—or possibly a combination of any of these. Some rich girls, especially in Europe, even have chapels in their homes or castles. It's here where they come and pray to meet the right poor boy. Of course, every rich girl's house has to have maids' rooms, servants' quarters, a butler's pantry, and at least one guest room for the visiting poor boy.

It would, of course, be impossible to describe *all* the towns and suburbs that shelter the rich girl, for she is, after all, a national, not a regional, phenomenon. There are, however, a few villages, towns, and suburbs which have a strong association with the rich girl, with which every poor boy should be familiar. I've been lucky and have visited them all. Soon you'll be hearing these names constantly and with some luck visiting them frequently. Let's discuss a few of these towns briefly. Remember, you want to go in and out the *front* door.

Bryn Mawr, Pennsylvania

Philadelphia's Main Line, a seventeen-mile-long stretch of venerable towns and villages like Haverford, Ardmore, and Gladwyne retains the allegiance of many rich Philadelphia families. It was here in the nineteenth century that many prominent families established magnificent estates along the Main Line of the Pennsylvania Railroad. Although the Main Line continues to represent a very conservative lifestyle, it can be the perfect place to enjoy the cultural life of Philadelphia and the athletic pursuits at the Merion Cricket Club, the Merion Golf Club, or the Radnor Hunt. For many poor boys, an extended visit to the Main Line has proven to be the most direct route to sharing the wealth of a rich girl's life.

Bryn Mawr, especially the "northside," seems to represent the best of the Main Line and boasts an excellent college long favored by rich girls; its shady neighborhoods suggest an aristocratic aloofness that I've always enjoyed. Don't be fooled, however—those Main Line girls are very, very approachable. I've met a few who were even accessible.

FAR HILLS, NEW JERSEY

Rich girls in New Jersey? You shouldn't be surprised. The Garden State has a number of villages, towns, and suburbs which shelter rich girls who are suitable for even the choosiest of poor boys. Although I've always welcomed weekends in Princeton and Rumson, it's the area surrounding Far Hills that's always had a special appeal for me.

Located approximately fifty miles west of New York City, this bucolic enclave of large estates, country homes, and very gentlemanly farms seems very much like England at times. Of course, in Far Hills it seems that absolutely everyone rides to the hounds: the Essex Fox Hounds.

Although the pastures, meadows, and open fields may seem a perpetual green, the most enduring color is found in the terribly blue-blooded residents of Far Hills and its neighboring communities. Families with names like Vance, Dillon, Brady, Scribner, Forbes, and Pierrepont claim this preserve as home, and many still live in greater manor houses or farms dating from the Revolutionary War period. It's a patriotic paradise every poor boy should explore.

GREENWICH, CONNECTICUT

Located only thirty-five miles from New York City, this town of 60,000 is a mix of new and old money. Greenwich remains, however, the home of some of America's wealthiest families. Daddy may be a private investor, a successful New York lawyer, or a chairman of the board waiting for his golden parachute to open. He probably commutes to New York by limousine or helicopter and certainly has a driver and/or pilot of his very own.

I'm advised by one female friend that the term "preppy" was invented here by former resident George Bush in 1953. Greenwich is very WASP and terribly preppy and has dozens of country clubs. I think of Greenwich as "high" prep. My favorite part of town is the "back-country," where magnificent homes and estates dot the rolling landscape. A lot of polo is played here, so bring your hard hat and riding gear. I always feel at home in Greenwich and hope that you will too.

GROSSE POINTE, MICHIGAN

This small enclave of privilege was a summer resort of Detroit's wealthiest families long before it became one of America's richest suburbs. It still seems like a resort to me. There are actually five Grosse Pointes: Grosse Pointe Farms, Grosse Pointe Park, Grosse Pointe Shores, Grosse Pointe Woods, and Grosse Pointe City. Grosse Pointe Farms is the very richest of the Grosse Pointes and almost everyone seems to have a pool, tennis court, and sailboat on Lake St. Claire. Residents here really don't need a country club.

Mummy and Daddy are probably descendants of automobile tycoons or families that made fortunes in timber, banking, or manufacturing. Expect to meet a lot of Fords since there are three distinct Ford families: the "salt" Fords, the "auto" Fords, and the "banking" Fords. Everyone seems related to a Ford. If you're lucky, you'll put a Ford in your life: you won't be the first poor boy who did.

The Poor Boy's Guide

HILLSBOROUGH, CALIFORNIA

South of San Francisco, on the long extension called the Peninsula, lie several enclaves that have sheltered rich girls for decades: Burlingame (the site of the first country club in California); the vast estates of Atherton; and the lush greenery and stables that typify more rustic Woodside. It's Hillsborough, however, that is the ultimate citadel of the rich San Franciscan. Patty Hearst used to live here.

This town, with a population of approximately 10,000, nestled in the hills above Burlingame, must be San Francisco's most elegant and expensive suburb. Its six square miles of manicured lawns and elaborate gardens separate mansion after mansion after mansion. I'm told that Hillsborough boasts more rich girls per square mile than any other town or suburb, which gives "population density" a new meaning.

I've heard of some poor boys who hyperventilate upon seeing this sumptuous town. I left breathless, for many reasons. I hope you're as fortunate.

LA JOLLA, CALIFORNIA

This town of 30,000 residents is officially part of San Diego but exists as a world unto itself. La Jolla occupies a small stretch of coastline fourteen miles north of San Diego. It's an elegant but comfortable beach town with magnificent homes and private clubs for almost every kind of activity. I visit the Beach and Tennis Club or the La Jolla Country Club with religious regularity. La Jolla's spectacular peninsula provides the poor boy with a magnificent panorama of California's greatest natural resource, the rich girl. La Jolla regularly attracts visitors from the Midwest, Texas, and other parts of California, so please book a flight early.

La Jolla's name is evidently derived from the Spanish word meaning jewel . . . and a jewel of California's coastline it is. Its breathtaking beaches, mild temperature, and abundance of rich girls make La Jolla a paradise for the poor boy.

LAKE FOREST, ILLINOIS

This town has long been considered among the wealthiest of Chicago's North Shore suburbs. It's sometimes called the "Greenwich of Chicago." Lake Forest is only about one hour from Chicago by train and is the home of many of Chicago's millionaires; names like Armour, Pullman, Field, Searle, and Donnelley are common. The telephone directory lists eight Armours alone, not including Mrs. Armour, who has separate phones in the "residence," the "garage," the "greenhouse," and the "pantry." I told you that rich girls like to eat well.

Lake Forest is a stunning town with magnificent homes overlooking wooded bluffs, deep ravines, and the sandy shores of Lake Michigan. I've met dozens of rich girls at elegant parties in mansions and on estates along Lake, Mayflower, or Sheridan Road. I've never left disappointed. Unfortunately, the winters here are very cold, so bring your longjohns and snowshoes. Don't worry though, these Midwest girls are terribly friendly, and they'll soon make every effort to warm you up.

LOCUST VALLEY, NEW YORK

The North Shore of Long Island boasts a number of affluent communities, which together are called the Gold Coast. They include Centre Island, Mill Neck, Matinecock, Lattingtown and Locust Valley, the capital of the Gold Coast. The villages around Locust Valley have many fine mansions, estates, and compounds, and a surplus of rich girls, many of whom can be found at the Piping Rock Club or the nearby Seawanhaka Corinthian Yacht Club on Centre Island. Absolutely everyone is listed in *The Social Register*.

The Poor Boy's Guide

Unfortunately, residents of Locust Valley suffer from one of the few diseases which only strike the rich: lockjaw. This disease originated in Locust Valley in the 1930s but has been spreading quickly ever since . . . wealthy folks as far west as Wayzata, Minnesota, and as far south as Chevy Chase, Maryland, have since been infected. The only known symptoms are wealth and difficulty in fully opening the mouth when speaking. Lockjaw is the social disease among East Coast rich girls and their Mummies and Daddies. There is no known cure. Thank God it's not fatal.

MANCHESTER, MASSACHUSETTS

A drive through Manchester, where splendid mansions rest among acres of landscaped gardens overlooking the sea, is a memorable experience. Down those long driveways live rich girls with names like Cabot, Lodge, Peabody, and Adams . . . Boston Brahmins waiting for the poor boy with an interest in a historic association.

Although Boston's North Shore stretches over one hundred miles, from Boston Harbor to Ipswich (world famous for its fried clams), *the* North Shore consists of more than ten miles of wealthy, walled, and WASP shoreline extending from Beverly's Woodbury Point, through the havens of Pride's Crossing and Beverly Farms, and ending at Manchester. These towns were initially conceived as summer retreats for Boston's elite, and they remain exclusive havens for Boston's dwindling blue bloods. Today these same towns are welcome apparitions for a poor boy who dreams of marrying a very proper, distinguished (and rich) Bostonian.

NEWPORT BEACH, CALIFORNIA

This attractive city south of Los Angeles is one of the oldest residential communities in Orange County and remains a seaside bastion of California society. Million-dollar homes line the shoreline of Harbor Island, Balboa Peninsula, Balboa Island, and Lido Isle, but it's the thousands of yachts which are the most accurate reflection of the wealth of this community. In fact, Newport Beach and Balboa boast over 10,000 pleasure crafts and the world's largest private harbor. I'm told that Newport Beach has some of the costliest slips in America; it's so very easy to believe. The whole area seems like one enormous yacht club . . . the perfect place for the poor boy who sails and wants to do much more. When visiting, I spend my time at the Newport Yacht Club.

Pleasure is one of the principal crafts of rich girls in Newport Beach . . . I've found that many a rich girl here will go down with her sail.

SOUTHPORT, CONNECTICUT

Farther up the Connecticut shore from Greenwich, this wealthy village is populated exclusively by WASP. Everyone seems to have blond hair and blue eyes. Even the maids are WASP.

Southport was once a bustling shipping and commercial steel center and boasts a small, but beautiful harbor which separates the town from a magnificent golf course. Today, the harbor is filled with pleasure boats of all sizes, and the once busy warehouses form part of the prestigious Pequot Yacht Club. The Greek Revival, Federal, and Victorian houses lining Harbor Road are now occupied by rich Mummies and Daddies and their equally affluent daughters. Sailing and golf (at least during the summer) are the principal activities; reading *The Wall Street Journal* and clipping coupons (cashing dividend checks) are the principal activities during winter. I try and visit Southport regularly. It's a perfect place to call "home."

TUXEDO PARK, NEW YORK

North of New York City and the steel and concrete canyons of Manhattan lies Westchester County and the cool, verdant, and exclusive oases of Purchase, Bedford, Bronxville, and Scarsdale. Each of these towns and villages claim an abundance of rich girls,

Tuxedo Park: it's a fortress definitely worth conquering.

and all merit the serious attention of the poor boy. My favorite citadel of the rich girl, however, remains Tuxedo Park. It's a fortress definitely worth conquering.

This walled enclave of 5,000 acres was originally conceived as a club and hunting preserve for wealthy Daddies during the 1880s. It has been a great success ever since. The tuxedo (or dinner jacket) made its American debut here in 1886 at the first Tuxedo Ball; it has since, of course, become the evening uniform of rich Daddies and society boys. The residents of Tuxedo Park all appear uniformly rich. Tuxedo Park, in fact, exists as a very quiet and very private retreat. One of my best friends insists that Tuxedo is one of the few places where rich girls can live simply, albeit elegantly. I've always been in favor of the simple life, haven't you?

Home Sweet Home

WAYZATA, MINNESOTA

This town lies on the shore of Lake Minnetonka, which because of its dozens of capes, bays, and inlets is often considered among the most beautiful lakes in Minnesota. Here the Sioux and the Chippewa worshiped the Great Spirit, Manitou, ruler of the waters of Me-ne-a-ton-ka. Today, poor boys from throughout the Midwest travel to worship a different spirit—the rich Wayzata girl.

For Wayzata, initially conceived as a resort in the nineteenth century, is now home for many of Minnesota's richest families, including the Pillsburys, Peaveys, MacMillans, and Daytons.

Daddy may be an heir to a great grain and trading fortune, a prominent industrialist, or a millionaire financier. Although winters are unusually long and cold, every conceivable effort is made to keep visitors (especially poor boys) warm. My own experience suggests that the rich Wayzata girl has a spirited imagination.

I'm told by a close friend that more rich girls have been married in the Wayzata Community Church and St. Martin's by the Lake than in any other churches west of the Mississippi. Who can doubt it?

Since the rich girl's home is so important to her life, I suggest that the serious reader do independent research. Every poor boy would profit by subscriptions to both *Architectural Digest* and *House & Garden*. Both publications provide inside views of the rich girl's home and constant reminders of what sharing the wealth will ultimately mean. Remember, you'll be sharing this life (and house) someday, so get acquainted with it early.

Other Towns of Note

Since the rich girl is a national, not a regional, phenomenon, the poor boy can discover her throughout the country; she is, after all, a national resource. Here's a partial list of other towns, suburbs, and cities which have a high rich girl per capita ratio.

Ardmore, PA	Metairie, LA (Northline Ave.)
Atherton, CA	Midland, TX
Barrington Hills, IL	Minnetonka, MN
Bedford, NY	Mission Hills, KN
Bellevue, WA	New Canaan, CT
Beverly Farms, MA	North Oak, MN
Birmingham, MI	Pasadena, CA
Bloomfield Hills, MI	Pride's Crossing, MA
Burlingame, CA	Princeton, NJ
Chevy Chase, MD	Purchase, NY
Clayton, MO	Rumson, NJ
Darien, CT	Ruxton, MD
Dunwoody, GA	Santa Barbara, CA
Fox Chapel, PA	Scarsdale, NY
Germantown, TN	Scottsdale, AZ
Haverford, PA	Shaker Heights, OH
Kenilworth, IL	Tiburon, CA
Ladue, MO	Tyler, TX
Lookout Mountain, TN	Victoria, TX
Los Gatos, CA	Wellesley, MA
McLean, VA	Winston-Salem, NC
Mercer Island, WA	Woodside, CA

Home Sweet Home

The Good Guest

You'll soon be spending a weekend as a house guest of at least one rich girl and her Mummy and Daddy. You want to be a good guest: both polite and popular. Let's hope that this will be the first of many, many invitations to Mummy and Daddy's mansion, estate, or compound; you do want to come again and again. Of course the first weekend may be your initial opportunity to meet Mummy and Daddy, and you especially want to make a very positive impression.

There are, as you can easily imagine, some important rules of behavior to observe when visiting the rich girl and her Mummy and Daddy. I want you to read the following carefully in preparation for those field trips to Wayzata, Far Hills, or La Jolla.

- Always bring a small house gift for Mummy. I suggest candy (especially expensive European chocolates), a book, or a bottle of Château Margaux.
- Pack appropriate clothing. Ask when invited whether you'll need a suit, black tie (tuxedo), opera slippers, etc.
- If you'll be visiting the country club or hunt club, bring your own riding outfit, tennis racquet, and golf clubs.
- Be prepared for anything. Visiting a rich girl's family can always be a surprise. Be flexible and enthusiastic no matter what the circumstances.
- Always act as if you're enjoying yourself . . . even if you're not.
- Don't break anything. If you do break something, volunteer to replace it.
- Never stay longer than invited. If you've been invited for a weekend, that means Saturday and Sunday. You're not living there permanently (at least not yet).
- When you retire for the evening (i.e., go to bed), stay in your bed. Midnight "wanderings" and rendezvous are highly discouraged. Sleepwalking is no excuse.

*When visiting the rich girl,
be sure to come prepared.*

- Don't sleep late; Mummy and Daddy may think you're lazy. You want to leave them with the impression (true or not) that you're energetic.
- Always say "Please" and "Thank you."
- Ask how you should dress for dinner. Mummy and Daddy may *dress* for dinner. This means black tie!
- If you use the telephone, charge long-distance calls to your home phone or that of your parents. I'm sure they'll understand.
- Always address the staff by their proper names. Servants have become a major problem (especially finding and keeping them), so no matter how rich Mummy and Daddy are, don't expect a big staff. If the staff has recently quit, is on strike or on vacation, help out . . . make your own bed, help clean the dishes, and take the garbage out. You may end up doing all the work.
- If there is a large staff, let them work. Don't touch a thing.
- Leave a small gratuity for any member of the staff who has given

you personal service. Personal service includes ironing, polishing shoes, making your bed, and drawing a bath, *but* nothing more.
- Say "Thank you" when leaving . . . even if you don't want to. You may have second thoughts when you return to your studio apartment.

In the City

Some rich girls grow up in the city—whether the older, more geographically distinct cities of the East Coast and South or the sprawling cities of the West and Southwest. Mummy and Daddy may have a home (Dallas and Houston have fine residential neighborhoods), a townhouse (especially in Washington, Boston, or New York), or a duplex or triplex overlooking the "lake" or the "bay" (in Chicago and San Francisco). Wherever Mummy and Daddy live, their address is terribly important since you may end up living there as well. Let's review the "best" addresses of our largest cities individually:

in Atlanta:	Buckhead
in Baltimore:	Guilford
	Roland Park
in Birmingham:	Mountain Brook
in Boston:	Beacon Hill
in Chicago:	Gold Coast
	Streeterville
	Lake Shore Drive
in Dallas:	Highland Park
in Fort Worth:	Westover Hills
in Houston:	River Oaks

☞

in Kansas City:	Country Club District
in Los Angeles:	Beverly Hills
	Bel Air
	Malibu
in Memphis:	Shady Grove
in Miami:	Coral Gables
	Indian Creek Island
in Minneapolis:	Kenwood Area
in Nashville:	Belle Mead
in New Orleans:	Audubon Place
	Garden District
in New York:	Park and Fifth Avenues
	Sutton Place
	Beekman Terrace
in Oklahoma City:	Nichols Hills
in Philadelphia:	Society Hill
	Chestnut Hill
	Rittenhouse Square
in Pittsburgh:	Shadyside
in St. Louis:	Central West End
in San Antonio:	Alamo Heights
in San Francisco:	Nob Hill
	Russian Hill
in Seattle:	Broadmore
in Tulsa:	Southern Hills Country Club Area
in Washington:	Georgetown
	Foxhall Road
	Kalorama

Chapter Three

Mummy

All rich girls love their mothers, whom they usually call Mummy. There are three principal reasons why rich girls love Mummy. First Mummy *married* Daddy, who has a great deal of money and spends an increasing percentage of it on her. Second, Mummy has *inherited* a great deal of money and spends an increasing percentage of it on her. Third, Mummy has *made* a great deal of money and spends an increasingly large percentage of it on her. Yes, there are an increasing number of rich Mummies who contribute to the family fortune. (See "The Working Mummy," later in this chapter.)

The Great Example

Mothers have always attempted to set a fine example for their daughters to follow; Mummy is certainly no exception.

Mummy is a model mother of sorts: she's an advocate of etiquette, a defender of decorum, and a partisan of propriety. She's also an influential moral force for she's instilled high standards of judgment *and* comparison.

Mummy

Mummy's much more than a moral influence, however, since she's even responsible for establishing the rich girl's advanced state of taste in clothing (silk taffeta, Fendi furs, and crepe dinner dresses), jewelry, antiques (anything Chippendale, Regency, or French Provincial), and reading. Mummy is simply terribly influential.

Mummy is also largely responsible for the rich girl's values, goals, and expectations. She has certainly established patterns of behavior which the rich girl is likely to emulate. Mummy has not only explained the facts of life, the need to circulate and contribute, she has certainly done a lot of circulating and contributing herself.

Mummy

The Great Consoler

Mothers have always attempted to lessen or mitigate grief, sorrow, or the sudden distress of life's many personal disappointments, for mothers are instinctively warm and comforting, especially during a period of need or a personal crisis. Mothers are a source of solace. Mummy is no exception.

Mummy is supportive and sometimes even emotive; she's almost always willing to comfort and console her little rich girl. She's always there at the worst of times: whether it's the loss of a drop earring at the Palm Beach ball, a spot on the white silk and satin debutante dress, or a fall from her favorite horse. Mummy is always prepared to commiserate, whether it's the "disappointing" sale at Neiman's, the "terrible" menus at the country club, or the "disastrous" cut at the salon. Mummy has plenty of sympathy, and perhaps some empathy.

The Great Competitor

Mothers can be very competitive, for they all want the best for their children. Mummy is certainly no exception.

She not only wants the best, she expects it and gets it for herself as well as for her little rich girl. Daddy, after all, is the Great Provider and Mummy is very resourceful: she probably has a trust of her very own.

Some Mummies are prepared to spare no effort or expense to make a successful vertical ascent. Of course, she's never been concerned with keeping up with the Joneses; it's the Rockefellers, Murchisons, Fields, and Kennedys with whom she wants to compete.

Mummy is, therefore, very determined that her little girl receive the best in everything. This usually means private schools, hours of tennis, riding, and piano instructions, elegant holidays in Europe, and first-class travel everywhere.

The Poor Boy's Guide

Mummy's Interests

Mummy may or may not work (see "The Working Mummy" later in this chapter). Whatever her present employment status may be, Mummy maintains wide and varied interests which she pursues for pleasure, relaxation, or simply out of a deep feeling of social obligation. No matter what her motives may be, these interests often help define Mummy's personality, her social life, and her own goals, values, and expectations. They will certainly influence the perspective and behavior of her rich little girl. Mummy's interests, therefore, will be important not only to the rich girl but to you, the poor boy, as well.

Mummy as a Hostess

Mummy may be a highly esteemed hostess renowned for her dinner parties from coast to coast. Whether it's a barbecue for hundreds on the ranch in Kingsville, a black-tie dinner dance overlooking Lake St. Claire, or a simple Sunday supper at the family compound, her invitations are always in demand. Her dinner menus of smoked trout, endive, and raspberry *sorbet* and place settings of Limoges and Baccarat may appear in *Town & Country* or *Gourmet*. She's admired for her clever seating and her guest list may include presidents and chairmen of the board, as well as leading cultural figures like Calvin Klein, Leonard Bernstein, and Paloma Picasso.

Mummy as a Volunteer

Mummy is usually a true believer in the arts, research, or the diseases. She's truly patronizing and is committed to giving her time and money to as many charitable organizations and cultural institutions as possible. She's a member of boards and committees, and is constantly in the columns or on the phone coaxing and coercing her friends to attend benefits, balls, fashion shows, and galas. She contributes each and every day.

Mummy may even be a leading lady of charity, responsible for raising millions of dollars each and every year for her favorite disease.

*M*UMMY AS A *B*REEDER

Mummy may be a well-known breeder—not of children but horses. She may buy, breed, and even supervise the training and racing careers of her stable. Breeding requires a great deal of time, social contacts, and money (all of which Mummy has), together with perseverance, for not every stallion measures up. Mummy knows all about bloodlines and is an authority on broodmares, colts, fillies, geldings, yearlings, and thoroughbreds. Mummy knows a stud when she sees one.

*M*UMMY AS A *D*ECORATOR

Mummy may live in a mansion, a duplex, or triplex apartment in the city, or on a large country estate. Wherever she lives, she's perfected the art of creating a fine and fashionable room. She knows all the sources for antique furniture, Oriental or Aubusson carpets, porcelain lamps, and chinoiserie panels. She has her fabrics cut from a different cloth, and has hundreds of samples of Scalamdre damask and Brunschwig glazed chintz. She may spend endless hours fantasizing about her next acquisition: a French armoire, a Georgian four-poster, or a Chippendale love seat. Mummy would love to get carried away.

*M*UMMY AS A *D*RESSER

Mummy may be very, very well dressed. She may purchase tailored suits, silk dresses, and strapless evening gowns from collections by Dior, Ungaro, Chanel, Saint Laurent, or Givenchy, or she may

The Poor Boy's Guide

prefer to support her American friends Bill, Geoffrey, Mary, Oscar, or Donna. She may have a wardrobe insured for hundreds of thousands of dollars and certainly dreams of getting on the "best-dressed" list.

Mummy as a Public Figure

Mummy loves publicity, at least the right kind. She dreams of interviews and full-day sessions with famous photographers and waits to read her name in all the columns (see Chapter 8, "Sources of Introduction"). She's always willing to "open the house" to the right magazine . . . she knows how to put out a very special welcome mat.

Mummy

The Working Mummy

Some Mummies choose to work. Unlike the mothers of many of her less affluent peers, the rich girl's Mummy really doesn't need the weekly paycheck, a medical plan, or the ultimate promise of Social Security. After all, Mummy has Daddy's income and/or trusts and her own medical "specialist"; she's probably already socially secure. Instead, Mummy only seeks fulfillment and the chance to contribute. She's part of that silent minority, the quiet rich, and still supports the Protestant work ethic.

Of course, many Mummies follow unusual career paths: they start at the top of their profession. Whether it's through inheritance, personal contacts, a seat on the board, or simply natural ability, they seem born to be achievers. They're often overnight successes.

Here's a partial list of working Mummies, each of whom has raised at least one rich girl of her very own.

CAROLINA HERRERA: FASHION DESIGNER

Introduced to the famed courtier Balenciaga at an early age, Carolina has since developed a seamless reputation of her own in the fashion world. She specializes in the design of expensive ensembles for the rich and famous, whether silk satin pants, embroidered velvet jackets, puffed-sleeve taffeta gowns, or wedding dresses of organza and Belgian lace. Her collections are restrained but seductive, and thousands of Mummies and their daughters get in *and* out of her designs each and every day—sometimes with a helping hand from a poor boy.

DINA MERRILL: ACTRESS

The daughter of Marjorie Merriweather Post (see Chapter 7, "Legends") and E. F. Hutton reportedly grew up in a bedroom decorated like Sleeping Beauty's. Dina, however, has never been at rest, for she inherited her grandfather's (C. W. Post's) work ethic and her mother's love of the theater (together with many, many millions). Stage-struck at an early age, she graduated from George Washington University and enrolled at the American Academy of Dramatic Arts. Dina made her film debut in 1957 and has appeared in memorable film classics such as *Operation Petticoat, A Wedding,* and *Just Tell Me What You Want.* Dina never stops making dramatic appearances.

LEONORE ANNENBERG: DIPLOMAT

Although temporarily retired to Sunnylands, the vast Palm Springs estate she shares with her husband Walter Annenberg (owner of *TV Guide* and the *Philadelphia Enquirer*) and a priceless art collection, Lee remains a diplomat at heart. She did, of course, serve as U.S. Chief of Protocol, the most socially demanding of all jobs (see Chapter 10, "Choosing a Career"). Her appointment shattered the myth that the Reagan Administration had a sexual bias. In her spare time, she's offered social sanctuary to President Nixon, the Shah of Iran's family, members of the British royal family, and dozens of poor and society boys.

KATHARINE GRAHAM: EXECUTIVE

Katharine has been making headlines since the death of her husband, Philip Graham, in 1963, when she took control over the media company founded by her father. She owns and/or controls newspapers, TV stations, *The Washington Post,* and *Newsweek* magazine. Considered one of the richest and most powerful Mummies in America, Katharine has long been a role model for the rich girl with an interest in a publishing empire.

C. Z. Guest: Columnist

This dynamic member of New York society and mother of the "perpetual Deb," Cornelia Guest, writes a syndicated column on gardening that appears in a number of newspapers. An accomplished author, she's also published *C. Z. Guest's Garden Planner and Date Book,* a best-seller used by many rich Mummies. C. Z. is credited with the comeback of the tulip as a society flower and has introduced a generation of new readers to the floral world.

Barbara Howar: Correspondent

This writer, columnist, and correspondent for "Entertainment Tonight" had a well-earned reputation as Washington's most accommodating society hostess. A former debutante, her classic autobiography, *Laughing All the Way,* an insider's view of Washington, catapulted her to fame and fortune. Many rich girls watch Barbara every night.

Jacqueline Kennedy Onassis: Editor

This Vassar graduate and former wife of John F. Kennedy and Aristotle Onassis once worked as the "Inquiring Camera Girl" for the now defunct *Washington Times Herald.* After the untimely death of her second husband, she returned to the working world as a $200-per-week consulting editor for The Viking Press. Today she works long hours as an editor for rival publisher Doubleday, between riding with the Essex Hounds and visits to the Kennedy Compound, her estate on Martha's Vineyard, and Palm Beach. Jackie specializes in fashion, the decorative arts, and the lives of other rich girls.

The Poor Boy's Guide

ANNE COX CHAMBERS: EXECUTIVE

Long considered one of the ten richest women in the world, Anne's jobs have included serving as ambassador to Belgium, chairman of Atlanta Newspapers, and director of Cox Broadcasting Corp. An heiress like her contemporary Katharine Graham, Anne is a newsmaker every day and does so very profitably. In her spare time she's also a great contributor, with charitable interests ranging from the Museum of Modern Art to Ducks Unlimited (a sporting group dedicated to duck shooting). Like many rich girls, she attended Miss Porter's and Finch College.

CAROLINE HUNT SCHOELLKOPF: HOTELIER

This quiet and unassuming daughter of the legendary oil tycoon H. L. Hunt has recently turned to the hospitality business. Unlike her brothers, Nelson and Bunker, she has wisely diversified her financial interests; in fact she is considered the wealthiest woman in America by many. A sizable portion of her good fortune, once estimated in the billions, is invested for everyone to enjoy (at a price), for she's invested hundreds of millions from her trust (the Caroline Hunt Trust Estate) into luxury hotels under the auspices of Rosewood Hotels. She's proving night after night that no one can provide hospitality like a Hunt.

Mummy

Your Relationship with Mummy

You will want to develop a close and intimate relationship with Mummy. You want Mummy to approve of your prospects and encourage her little rich girl to encourage you. The quickest way to win a rich girl's heart (and money) is often through Mummy.

There are a number of rules of behavior that each and every poor boy should follow when building a close and enduring relationship with Mummy.

1. Never challenge Mummy. In many a rich girl's house, Mummy knows best.
2. Display honor and respect for Mummy and Mummy's many friends.
3. Constantly compliment Mummy:
   "Silk taffeta was made for you."
   "I love your chest." (Not *her* chest, the Regency chest.)
   "The Cancer Ball was a great success."
   "I enjoyed meeting Halston."
   "You photograph so well."
   "Maybe you should be a decorator."
4. When visiting always bring a house present, however small.
5. Mummy is committed to appearances. Always be neat, well groomed, and well dressed.
6. Never swear in front of Mummy.
7. Always praise Mummy's food (she may not have cooked it, but she probably chose the menu, the chef, or the caterer).
8. Always be prepared to discuss her varied interests, whether they include horse breeding, decorating, or the newest disease.

9. Dance with Mummy whenever you can, but *don't* hold her close.
10. Never interrupt Mummy. When Mummy speaks, everyone listens.

Dance with Mummy whenever you can,
but don't hold her close.

Mummy

Mummy's Best Friends

HER DEALER

Dealers don't sell a "foreign substance," although their very best merchandise is frequently imported. They do, however, sell Georgian furniture and silver from collapsing country houses, French commodes used by royal mistresses, and Flemish tapestries the size of billboards. Every major city and metropolitan area has dealers; in New York, it seems that there's a dealer on every corner.

The dealer meets Mummy for quiet lunches and teas where he describes his stock, his latest acquisitions, and his trips to London, Paris, and Rome. He's more than a confidante; he knows Mummy's taste *and* her favorite period.

HER HAIRDRESSER

Hair is central to much of Mummy's life. She's constantly being combed, cut, washed, and colored. Some Mummies even have a day cut and a night cut, and spend endless hours with their dresser discussing outfits, accessories, and color; Mummy can be very discriminating about her color.

Mummy has almost certainly developed a profound rapport with her dresser. They share many secrets over tints and conditioners.

HER DECORATOR

Whether its silk moiré draperies, chintz slipcovers, or floral prints, the decorator adds fabric to Mummy's life. The decorator knows that Mummy wants to live in style and helps her choose furniture, carpets, cabinets, and *objets d'art;* together they spend many afternoons planning color schemes, textures, lighting, and seating arrangements. The decorator knows how to put absolutely everything in its proper place, including Mummy.

The Poor Boy's Guide

Mummy's Hot Walker

The Hot Walker: he's a good dancer, an even better talker, and the very best walker (escort). He may be a dealer, a dresser, or a decorator, or simply an old and trusted family friend. He almost certainly is not married, and everyone assumes that he's a "confirmed" bachelor. He's probably an aging society boy who knows generations of rich girls; he may have walked hundreds, perhaps even thousands of rich girls.

*The most valuable part
of the Hot Walker's anatomy is his elbow.*

When Daddy's away (or simply too tired) and Mummy wants to play, the Hot Walker escorts Mummy to glamorous openings at the opera or ballet, elegant galas in gilded ballrooms, or dinner dances under pink-and-green-striped tents. The most valuable part

46

of the Hot Walker's anatomy is his elbow—it's the perfect place for Mummy to rest her weary arm. Of course the very best Hot Walkers provide mental as well as physical support—he's truly Mummy's very best friend.

I know one Hot Walker who claims to have walked the richest women in the world. He does have an enviable record: I've seen pictures of him with aging heiresses dressed in Ungaro, well-known breeders holding their cups, and famous queens taking a needed break from life at court. He makes frequent appearances in *W*, *Palm Beach Life*, all the gossip columns, and even *Vanity Fair*. He's a frequent guest at the White House and claims to have more black ties than any other man. He's confided to me that he's a "professional" Walker: it's his contribution to Society.

The Twelve Tribes

Mummy and Daddy may be members of one of the twelve tribes, each of which have certain customs, rituals, and patterns of dress that are virtually impossible to ignore. As members of a tribe, they may even espouse codes of behavior and values which they transmit from generation to generation.

The Super-Rich: This tribe is very small (members number in the hundreds) and very dispersed. They appear together annually in *Forbes* magazine.

The Old Rich: Members of this tribe are distinguished by the duration of their wealth: they made money long before any of the other tribes. There are major camps in Boston, Philadelphia, and New York, although some members adhere to tribal practices as far away as Chicago and San Francisco.

The Nouveau Riche: This tribe is recently rich and still can't believe it. The nation's most aggressive tribe, they fiercely and conspicuously display every sign of being rich.

The Jewish Rich: Typically a Reform tribe, they are strict adherents to the gold standard. They have major outposts in New York and Los Angeles.

The WASP Rich: The country's largest tribe. Although geographically dispersed, they continue to set standards for other tribes to follow. They gather weekly at campsites called country clubs. ☞

The Orange County Rich:	A new and very colorful tribe; they've smoked peace pipes (and presumably a lot more) with the Nouveau Riche and the Jewish Rich.
The Quiet Rich:	The lost tribe. Whatever happened to the Quiet Rich?
The New York Rich:	A very self-possessed tribe. Members of this tribe remain convinced that they represent the very best in every tribal custom. Of course, New York remains the melting pot, as other tribal members are quickly and quietly absorbed.
The Main Line Rich:	Members of this tribe reside in Philadelphia and the nearby suburbs of the Main Line. Blood brothers of the WASP Rich and Old Rich, they take Philadelphia very seriously.
The Texas Rich:	A very special tribe; in fact, they think that they're the *only* tribe. Members display dress and rituals normally associated with the Nouveau Riche.
The Catholic Rich:	Major camps in Boston, New York, and Chicago. Ironically members of this tribe are particularly devoted to the Protestant work ethic. Many members have pitched their tents as close as possible to members of the WASP tribe.
The Euro Rich:	A predominantly Continental tribe, although a few British are included. Members enjoy socializing with the Super-Rich and the Old Rich, and pretend that they're both.

Chapter Four

Daddy

*A*ll rich girls love their fathers, whom they usually call Daddy. There are three principal reasons why rich girls love Daddy. First, Daddy has *made* a great deal of money and spends an increasing percentage of it on her. Second, Daddy has *inherited* a great deal of money and spends an increasing percentage of it on her. Third, Daddy *married* Mummy, who has a great deal of money, and he spends an increasing percentage of Mummy's money on her.

The rich girl's deep emotional attachment to Daddy normally transcends her love for everything else, including her diamonds, clothes, and even Mummy and Nanny. After all, he's the principal man in her life until she meets the right poor boy. That's you.

THE GREAT PROVIDER

No matter how Daddy has acquired his fortune—through his own efforts, those of his Daddy, or those of Mummy's Daddy— he is and will remain the Great Provider. With some luck and hard work, you, the poor boy, will be the Great Provider someday. You'll be fortunate enough to have the resources to shelter your

Daddy

own little rich girl, and Mummy too. This is your ultimate goal.

Since Daddy has so much money, he can be very generous and almost always is. He sends his little rich girl to the very best schools, pays for frequent trips to Europe and idyllic Caribbean retreats, and covers the monthly bills at Neiman-Marcus, Bergdorf's, and I. Magnin. Even when the rich girl grows up (i.e., leaves home), he continues in this magnanimous role. Once you've found the right rich girl, you'll be the direct beneficiary of his generosity. Never refuse a helping hand from Daddy.

Daddy

The Poor Boy's Guide

The Great Protector

Fathers have always attempted to protect their daughters from the harsh realities of everyday life. Daddy is certainly no exception. He wants his own little rich girl to avoid the mundane trials and tribulations that affect her less affluent peers. The rich girl, therefore, is uniquely sheltered. She is raised behind large hedges and stone walls, attends private schools with other rich girls, and enjoys her summers and winters in exclusive retreats with old (and rich) family friends.

You never want to assume the role of taking the rich girl away from Daddy's protective umbrella. Instead, *you're trying to get out of the rain as well.*

The Great Decision Maker (Father Knows Best)

Because of Daddy's enormous wealth and power, he usually is very worldly and knows precisely what is best for his own rich little girl. He is full of compelling advice regarding schools, careers, friends, living arrangements, and even vacations. He will certainly have an opinion on you and your Prospects, and a positive one is crucial, since the rich girl rarely defies Daddy (at least not for long).

If you're to cultivate a warm relationship with Daddy, you need as much information as possible on his occupation, his interests, and his background. I've been introduced to hundreds of Daddies and, of course, have a father of my very own. Let's examine Daddy's occupation first, since, whether he works or not, he's probably fully employed.

Daddy

Daddy's Occupation

Daddy may or may not work since his financial resources or those of Mummy provide for the real security every poor boy seeks. Every Daddy that I've met has been committed to expanding the family fortune and contributing and thereby ensuring his own place in posterity. Of course, you want Daddy to continue to succeed, for your ultimate goal is a share in his success.

PHILANTHROPIST

Daddy is so rich that he insists on giving money away. Some Daddies have museums, hospitals, and dormitories named after them, while others endow "chairs" at leading universities or colleges. Some Daddies even have entire colleges or universities named after them (Daddies Duke, Vanderbilt, and Post did).

Of course, philanthropy is terribly smart, since it's designed to save money and avoid taxes. It's the rich Daddy's version of a standard deduction! Daddy's generosity is very impressive and usually a sign of very old money. Some social critics insist that old money is better than new money. *The currency has always been the same to me; it's usually just the people who are so terribly different.*

PRIVATE INVESTOR

Daddy is self-employed and he manages his money, Mummy's money, and a variety of family trusts. He usually spends the day on the telephone with his many investment advisers and brokers, checking movements in the market, "rallies," his "positions," and "tips." He follows the "tape" and knows all the bulls and bears. You have to ensure that he's as bullish on your Prospects as he is on the market.

The Poor Boy's Guide

Venture Capital

Daddy invests in new companies, usually high-tech or start-up ventures, producing chips, disks, and drives. If the venture succeeds, the company goes public and Daddy doubles, triples, or even quadruples his initial investment. You're engaged in a very personal venture as well; it's just the capital you lack.

Your own investment in this venture will include champagne, a classic refrigerator, and an acceptable wardrobe, all of which contribute to your Prospects.

Investment Banker

Daddy raises capital (i.e., vast amounts of money) for very large companies, cities, and even governments. He's a very powerful financial figure and is constantly pursued for his advice and counsel.

My counsel is simple and straightforward: use *The Guide* and you'll be raising capital quickly and economically. You'll never be dependent on a banker again.

Real Estate

Many Daddies made their money in real estate. Inflation has made many a Daddy a multimillionaire, while depreciation keeps the I.R.S. away. Trump, Taubman, and Mackel are just a few of the many important real-estate developers. I used to date a girl whose Daddy was a developer; he gave her a shopping center for Christmas.

The U.S. Senate

Now called the Millionaires' Club. Names like Kennedy, Heinz, Weicker, Danforth, and Bentsen suggest that the Senate cloakroom has become the "hot" profession for the rich Daddy. It's certainly a closet with many family skeletons.

Daddy

PERSONALITY

Entertainment is big business, and actors, athletes, and performers receive enormous paychecks. Some even get residuals: they perform once and keep on getting paid. Of course, when you marry the right rich girl, you'll be asked for more than just one performance.

CHIEF EXECUTIVE OFFICER (FORTUNE 100)

There is money in the corporate world today. Executives of many of the country's largest companies receive total compensation in excess of one million dollars annually. They not only receive salaries, they get "bonuses," "options," and "shares," all of which make the life of the C.E.O. very appealing. Of course many corporate executives daydream of getting a golden parachute: they land very safely and securely when their company is acquired, and they receive severance pay of ten to thirty million dollars. Then they become either philanthropists or private investors.

OIL

Many members of the Forbes 400 made their money in oil and natural gas. Of course, the Getty, Hunt, and Rockefeller dynasties all started through drilling or exploring. You'll be doing both very soon. Thank God for the Pleistocene era. Things are a bit rocky in oil these days, though, so move cautiously.

Daddy's Favorite Schools

Some self-made Daddies didn't go to school at all; others attended college for just a short time before they picked an occupation or married a rich Mummy. The majority of Daddies whom I have met, however, attended a few select schools:

Amherst College
C.C.N.Y. (only in New York, the Jewish Daddy)
Columbia University
Dartmouth College
Davidson College
Duke University
Georgetown University (the Catholic Daddy)
Harvard College
New York University
Northwestern University
Princeton University
Stanford University
University of Chicago
University of Michigan
University of Texas
University of Virginia
Vanderbilt University
Washington and Lee University
Wesleyan College
Williams College
Yale University

Daddy

Your Relationship with Daddy

Building and consolidating a warm and enduring relationship with Daddy is critical if you are to succeed in this elevating endeavor. Daddy will want to approve of both you and your Prospects; if he likes you a great deal, he will "encourage" his little rich girl and let her know that he thinks you're just the right boy for her. He'll even welcome you with open arms into the family compound, mansion, or estate. If you follow the following rules of behavior, Daddy can be your ultimate ally and benefactor.

1. Never argue with Daddy.
2. Display quiet admiration for Daddy.
3. Always volunteer. Examples:
   "May I bring in the sail?"
   "May I walk the ponies?"
   "May I call your broker?"
   "May I give you a stock tip?" (Be careful.)
   "May I pay for dinner?"
4. Act yourself and don't pretend. Daddy knows you're poor and really doesn't care as long as your Prospects are good.
5. Never talk about sex.
6. Never eat or drink too much.
7. Be cautious with money.
8. Always have money.
9. Be modest.
10. Remember that with some luck you'll be in Daddy's shoes (not to mention house, yacht, and Rolls) someday: you'll be the Great Protector and the Great Provider.

The Yacht Club

Daddy may spend many weekends at the yacht club where he moors his sloop, yawl, or ketch. I've always found that Daddies like to sail, while many society boys prefer to cruise.

I've always believed that there were many parallels between sailing and courting and marrying the right rich girl. Sailing requires an understanding of a specialized terminology (e.g., come about, jib, tack) and can be an unpredictable sport. Many enthusiasts find that sailing is a romantic endeavor and a physical challenge which can provide excitement as well as tranquility. (Finding the right rich girl would certainly give me peace of mind.) Sailing, however, does offer a great sense of personal fulfillment and achievement, and, like marrying the rich girl, it can be a way of life and an immensely rewarding experience.

I've spent many weekends with Daddy at the yacht club and encourage you to do precisely the same. If the winds of fortune blow your way, you may sail off with a catch of your very own: his little rich girl.

Here's a partial list of yacht clubs which I've sailed from:

New York Yacht Club	New York, New York
Seawanhaka Corinthian Yacht Club	Centre Island, New York
Chicago Yacht Club	Chicago, Illinois
Newport Yacht Club	Newport Beach, California
Larchmont Yacht Club	Larchmont, New York
Grosse Pointe Yacht Club	Grosse Pointe, Michigan
Eastern Yacht Club	Marblehead, Massachusetts
Ida Lewis Yacht Club	Newport, Rhode Island
American Yacht Club	Rye, New York
St. Francis Yacht Club	San Francisco, California
San Diego Yacht Club	San Diego, California
Little Traverse Yacht Club	Harbor Springs, Michigan

Chapter Five
Major Events in a Rich Girl's Life

*I*n order to understand the rich girl intimately, every poor boy must be well acquainted with those events that shape her life and determine her values, goals, expectations, and behavior. When one considers the rich girl, familiarity doesn't breed contempt; instead it breeds a poor boy with good Prospects, prepared to meet, court, and marry the right rich girl. Someday he'll share these values and a great deal more, for sharing the wealth is the ultimate objective of every poor boy. It's a social obligation, *noblesse oblige* and upward mobility in its purest sense.

You already know that the rich girl resides in a very special and, at times, very exclusive and mysterious world. If the rich girl is so different from her less affluent peers, it's largely because she has had a series of unique experiences which truly distinguish her. These shared experiences also account, to a great degree, for the close ties that rich girls have with one another and with society boys.

There are *six* major events in a rich girl's life. Although these events have been discussed *separately* in many articles and books,

The Poor Boy's Guide

this will be the first time the crucial six have been discussed together in one serious publication. Every poor boy will want to read this chapter slowly and with the utmost care.

Let's begin with Nanny, since she's so critical in understanding the rich girl's very unusual childhood.

The Death of Nanny

Some social critics claim that, together with the raincoat, roast beef, and Noël Coward, the English nanny is the major legacy of British civilization. I can't disagree. Personally I'm convinced that the English nanny has had a profound effect on the development of the American social system and on the behavior of the rich girl in particular. She's certainly affected the many rich girls that I've come to know.

Although originally intended as a nursemaid, the English nanny has historically become much, much more. In Edwardian England, where domestic service was the largest single source of employment, Nanny became a surrogate for Mummy and Daddy, who frequently traveled to London, the Continent, and what many still considered "the colonies." Nanny emerged as a powerful *ex-officio* member of the family, with responsibilities and prerogatives which often eclipsed those of Mummy and Daddy. Nanny established the eating, reading, sleeping, and lifelong social habits of her charges. She was, in short, a terribly influential person.

The rich girl's Nanny is a direct descendant of this important English tradition. As the American upper classes sought to emulate British society, especially the aristocracy, they imported English nannies. The practice continues today. (In Texas and California some families prefer Mexican or Philippine nannies; personally I'm convinced that Nanny, like the raincoat, was meant to be a British import.)

Like her European counterparts, the rich American girl was often terribly dependent on Nanny. For many a rich girl, Nanny seemed just like Mummy and Daddy, and she was frequently the

60

first person with whom the rich girl developed a close emotional attachment. Nanny was often the first person to bathe and dress her, admonish and praise her.

Nanny took the rich girl for long strolls down Fifth Avenue or Lake Shore Drive and built castles in the sand with her at Newport, Sea Island, La Jolla, or Southampton. In the winter Nanny would usually stay home with her while Mummy and Daddy traveled to Palm Beach or the Other Palm. She was a source of companionship, love, and welcome advice.

Since Nanny is much older than either Mummy or Daddy, the death of Nanny is usually the rich girl's first loss of a family member. It's a traumatic event, one which she rarely forgets. I always inquire about Nanny and have learned to listen patiently to tender and often moving stories about how special each rich girl's Nanny was. You'll want to do the same, for with some luck, your own offspring will someday have a Nanny of their very own.

Nanny—a source of companionship,
love, and welcome advice.

The Poor Boy's Guide

HER FIRST TRIP TO PALM BEACH

Legend has it that Palm Beach owes its existence to the shipwreck of a Spanish cargo ship in the 1870s. This ill-fated vessel was laden with thousands of coconuts, which, floating to the nearby beach, gradually developed into the majestic palms which line this island's shoreline and give Palm Beach its now world-renowned name. Years later these same palms attracted the attention of railroad magnate Henry M. Flagler, who wanted to develop a great Florida resort. Fortunately, he succeeded admirably, and Palm Beach became the winter version of Newport, Rhode Island, soon attracting America's wealthy and socially prominent to its breathtaking shores. Today Palm Beach retains the allegiance of many of the wealthy in this country and abroad. It is the *grande dame* of all winter resorts.

From December through March, Palm Beach becomes a veritable mecca for rich Mummies and Daddies from around the world. It also becomes a winter playground for many rich girls (see Chapter 12, "The Flight into Palm Beach"). No other winter retreat can boast the concentration of wealth and the absolute numbers of Mummies, Daddies, and rich girls that Palm Beach shelters. The season here is *the* social reason. No other city or town offers any serious competition.

Since Palm Beach is so terribly special, the rich girl's first visit there takes on great significance. This first trip includes introductions to a number of very rich and very famous Seniors (the very Senior—i.e., over seventy—adore Palm Beach). She'll be introduced to other rich girls and will meet notorious society boys who've escorted movie stars, heiresses, and even queens. She will shop along Worth Avenue, spend leisurely afternoons reading catalogues at the Everglades Club, and dine and dance at Mediterranean mansions with Spanish names along Ocean Boulevard. It will be an overwhelming experience, and one that very few girls her age will ever share.

Major Events in a Rich Girl's Life

The first visit to Palm Beach, therefore, provides a valuable perspective for the rich girl and another clue to how very special her world actually is. She'll return home healthier, happier, and wiser, secure in knowing that she's made new friends and that she has a winter place to go to.

Her Coming Out

Rich girls don't come out of closets, although some society boys do. Instead, they come out, or more accurately, are presented, at cotillions, assemblies, balls, and debutante parties at large hotels and private clubs. Alternatively, some rich girls have private parties under yellow- or green-striped tents on Mummy and Daddy's estate or at the family compound. Whatever the venue, coming out is a major event in almost every rich girl's life.

A number of historians insist that this social custom has tribal origins, and cite African and Polynesian rituals and ceremonies. Some anthropologists even suggest that the modern debutante ball can be traced to prehistory. Although some debutantes may at first seem primitive, the present custom is most likely Continental in origin, for during the seventeenth and eighteenth centuries, European monarchs began the practice of requiring that eligible young women be presented at court in lengthy and elaborate ceremonies. To be invited to court was soon viewed as a privilege and was relished as an opportunity to display the family's wealth, power, and position in society. This presentation or debut ultimately became a rite of passage from puberty to marriage, an essential stop on the rich girl's journey from adolescence to adulthood.

Today's debutante is a rich girl in her late teens, probably a freshman in college. Mummy has probably planned her debut for a year or more—sometimes even years, since a few cotillions and assemblies are very, very popular and waiting lists are not uncommon. Some Mummies even insist on several debuts; their little rich girls come out at parties in cities across the country throughout the season. It can be a very expensive affair. I know one Mummy who spent hundreds of thousands on her little rich girl's debut. It was an unforgettable event; even the network news provided live coverage.

Coming Out Tonight

This following list is not designed to be inclusive, but these balls, cotillions, and assemblies are among the most exclusive debutante parties for the rich girl. Get invited and be an escort if you possibly can.

Atlanta	The Phoenix Ball
	Halloween Ball
Baltimore	Bachelor's Cotillion
Beverly Hills	The Evergreen Ball
Birmingham	Redstone Debutante Ball
Boston	Cotillion Ball
Charleston	Saint Cecilia Ball
Chicago	Passavant Cotillion
Cincinnati	The Bachelor's Cotillion
Columbia	The Assembly
Dallas	Idlewild Ball
Denver	The Debutante Ball
Fort Worth	The Assembly
	Steeplechase Ball
Houston	Allegro Ball
Kansas City	Jewel Ball
Los Angeles	Las Madrinas Debutante Ball
Louisville	The Debutante Ball
Miami	Surf Club Debutante Ball

☞

Major Events in a Rich Girl's Life

Nashville	Eve of Janus Ball
New Orleans	Mardi Gras (Rex, Comus, Momus)
New York	Junior Assembly
	International Debutante Ball
	New York Infirmary Ball
	New York Junior League Ball
	New York Debutante Cotillion &
	Christmas Ball
Philadelphia	Philadelphia Assemblies
Pittsburgh	Cinderella Ball
Raleigh	Terpsichorean Ball
Richmond	Richmond German
St. Louis	Fleur de Lis Ball
	Veiled Prophet Ball
San Antonio	The Germans
San Francisco	San Francisco Cotillion
Washington, D.C.	International Debutante Ball
	The Christmas Ball
	National Debutante Ball
Wilmington	Holly Ball

The debutante season usually begins in late autumn, often around Thanksgiving, and reaches a crescendo during Christmas week, when rich girls throughout the country take their bows at private clubs and gilded ballrooms. It's a Christmas gift for poor boys. Of course, some rich girls prefer to come out in late May or early June before they leave for the Fertile Crescent (see Chapter 11) or other summer resorts. It's a great summer send-off.

I've always enjoyed debutante parties. They are tremendous fun and an invitation should never, ever be refused, since, of course, the debutante party is one of the best ways of networking. They can, however, be exhausting, especially if you're lucky enough to be an escort for one of the debutantes.

Most assemblies, cotillions, and debutante balls begin in the early evening and often extend into the early hours of the following morning. The party usually begins with drinks, and hors d'oeuvres for all the Mummies and Daddies, the other family members, and invited guests in the grand ballroom or the main room of the country club. It's a perfect occasion for fingering, as everyone is eating with their hands. At the largest cotillions and assemblies (where forty or more rich girls may come out), the guest list may number five hundred or more.

The rich girl and her escort(s) wait nervously in the wings for the actual presentation to begin. As the guests are seated and the lights dim, the band or orchestra begins to play: the evening has started. Each girl (who has at least one escort and maybe two) enters the stage of the grand ballroom. Her name and those of her Mummy and Daddy are announced, her escort is introduced, and then, in the sudden silence of the grand ballroom, with flash-bulbs flickering . . . she bows. It's a grand entrance especially designed with the rich girl in mind. The evening ends with dancing, dinner, and probably a breakfast at a rich girl's mansion, estate, or compound. It's quite an intoxicating affair.

Rich girls don't come out of closets, although some society boys do.

Major Events in a Rich Girl's Life

I've been an escort on many occasions, and it never ceases to be an exciting and enchanting experience. I've known a few escorts (presumably jealous of the attention the debutantes command) to discreetly whisper that they wish they were coming out. Many do later on.

Her First Trust

The rich girl is probably the beneficiary of at least one trust fund. Trusts have been used by rich Mummies and Daddies for generations to maintain property, to provide for spending money, and to limit and even to avoid inheritance taxes.

Many rich girls are born with a trust fund; for others one is established at an early age. Some receive a trust fund at sixteen, others at twenty-one. Some girls have several trust funds or share trust funds with members of their immediate family. Rich girls that have enormous trusts are called heiresses. The heiress is the right rich girl for the overachiever.

Although there are all kinds of trusts, the most important concept for every poor boy to remember is that income from a trust permits the rich girl to purchase things that her less affluent peers ordinarily can never afford. The trust fund literally sets her apart. Trusts also show how inventive the rich (and their many lawyers) can be. With some luck and proper planning, you'll be a beneficiary of a trust some day.

In many cases the rich girl receives only income from her trust and can never use the principal. In other instances she gradually assumes control over the property, bank accounts, oil wells, and shares of stock which comprise her trust. It all sounds very complicated and is, for the creation and management of trusts is a major preoccupation of the legal profession. Many, many lawyers specialize in trusts and estates; it's one of the principal reasons we *have* a legal profession.

The trust, whatever its limitations, does provide the rich girl with a constant source of income. Although Mummy and Daddy may send her checks or gifts, the trust fund gives the rich girl a great degree of independence and the freedom to circulate and contribute.

Never ask a rich girl about her trusts directly. Don't worry, she'll usually volunteer information about this (her most vital statistic) after at least one perfect date. Listen carefully!

HER FIRST MINK (PICKING THE PELTS)

Rich girls wear mink. The rich girl traditionally purchases her first mink or receives it as a gift from Mummy and Daddy during her mid to late twenties. It is her first major piece of Senior, or adult, clothing and is designed to keep her warm between visits to Palm Beach.

The rich girl usually visits several furriers before choosing her pelts. Although she may purchase a mink off the rack, many rich girls prefer to have coats made especially for them. In this case, the pelts or skins of the mink are often chosen individually by the rich girl and her Mummy at her furrier. Although pelts from the male mink are bushier and bigger than the female mink's, the best mink coats are made from female pelts. Some rich girls sign each pelt to ensure it goes in her coat and not in some other rich girl's. A full-length, collared mink has a minimum of thirty pelts, so picking the pelts is a long and challenging job. It's also a great deal of fun.

A famous furrier (he's clothed thousands of rich girls) claims that the rich girls and the mink are very much alike. The mink, after all, is at home on water and on land, and is nocturnal by nature. Minks are skilled swimmers and divers and, when angry, are known to sometimes spit and squeal with rage. A good mink coat, like the right rich girl, can last forever. The mink coat's worst enemy is the car seat, especially the back seat. I know several poor boys who started out in the back seat and ended up in the driver's seat.

Major Events in a Rich Girl's Life

All the rich girls I've known also have a fur muff. These are very warm inside.

Her First Swim

The rich girl traditionally joins her first swim, or social circle, after college. The swim will influence her choice of friends and interests, and perhaps even her selection of a husband. The rich girl's prep school is designed to instill a sense of community with other rich girls and boys, while, of course, establishing her basic knowledge of French, art, music, and field hockey. College, in contrast, widens the rich girl's world—she finally meets poor boys. This can be a traumatic, although rewarding, experience. Once the initial shock disappears, however, the rich girl is forced to assess her life and compare it with those of her less affluent peers. Gradually, often reluctantly, she accepts her privileged fate and begins to appreciate how truly different her life is destined to be. It's self-acceptance in its most basic form.

The swim returns the rich girl to her very special and exclusive world. The swim is a social circle usually limited to other rich girls, rich boys, and society boys—its exclusivity is purely accidental and certainly not by design. Members of a swim share many common experiences, for they have probably summered, prepped, come out, and sailed together. Their interests, goals, and even trusts may be the same.

Entering a swim is a major event for every rich girl, since many of the *swells* (members) will become lifelong friends, confidantes, and companions . . . and for some, husbands. Certain swims are based on the summer season (there are Southampton, La Jolla, Newport, and Maine swims); other swims center on common prep schools and at least a few are based on colleges (e.g., the Ivy swims). Alternatively, some swims are based on interests in sports, especially polo and sailing, or revolve around professions: the art and antique swims for instance. Members of a swim eat together, attend benefits together, travel together, and may have sex together. Sometimes they even *swim* together.

Years later, when the rich girl has married (hopefully you), she will leave her swim for a tribe. Tribes are composed of very social Seniors who have enormous social, political, and economic power.

Joining a swim should be a primary objective of every poor boy: learning how to swim (i.e., circulate) is a great deal of fun. The more you swim, the happier and healthier you'll be and the better your Prospects will be.

MEETING YOU

Yes, meeting you may be the most important event in a rich girl's life. Whether through a casual meeting in the classroom or at the polo game, a dance at the Palm Beach Ball, or while planning seating at a benefit committee meeting, every introduction to a rich girl is a significant social event for both of you. Remember, although a rich girl's trusts, cottage in Newport or Sea Island, prep school, and swim elevates her above all others, every girl, rich and poor alike, secretly shares the same goal: meeting the right boy. That's you.

Every time I meet an attractive rich girl, I immediately recognize that this could be the right rich girl for me. I realize that this introduction could lead to many perfect dates, a swim, visits to the Fertile Crescent (see Chapter 11), and sex with the rich girl. Most importantly it could lead to a proposal and marriage. I've developed a powerful and positive mind set and want you to do the very same. I expect the best out of life and believe that if you expect the best that you'll ultimately achieve it. I, therefore, believe in the natural corollary: expect to marry a rich girl and you will.

In fact, whenever I meet a rich girl I always think positive. The positive poor boy never dwells on the negative (his singular handicap . . . being poor) but instead always concentrates on the bright future which may lie ahead: sharing the wealth of a rich girl's life.

Chapter Six
❧
Special Situations

$\mathscr{T}$he rich girl is, above all, a product of circumstance. The word "circumstance" implies "to whom you were born," which clearly is beyond the control of even the richest of girls. Whether it's the silver spoon, the trust fund, or the title that sets her apart, her circumstances are dramatically different from her less affluent peers. It's precisely your present circumstances that we're about to change.

There are, of course, also geographic, historic, and social circumstances that account for some differences (however minor) among rich girls themselves. These differences result in special situations which require the serious attention of each and every poor boy. I've always found that special situations are particularly appealing; they offer a wealth of opportunity for the knowledgeable poor boy. Let's investigate a few special situations which you may someday encounter.

THE PARK RANGER

She's a very special breed of rich girl who has adapted her lifestyle to the steel canyons and concrete sidewalks of the nation's largest city, New York. She's definitely an urban creature and lives in a co-op, condominium, or townhouse on Manhattan's Upper East Side. Although she may venture to distant places like "SoHo," "the Village," or "the West Side," her natural territory is a narrow corridor two blocks east and two blocks west of Manhattan's famous Park Avenue. She's called a Park Ranger.

She travels up and down this wide boulevard dozens of times each day on excursions to the nearby Tiffany's, Bergdorf's, and

Favorites of the Park Ranger

Favorite Street:	Park Avenue
Favorite Restaurant:	Mortimer's
Favorite Bank:	Morgan Guaranty
Favorite Benefit:	Anything for Sloane-Kettering
Favorite Drink:	Kir Royale
Favorite Senior:	Pat Buckley
	(Mrs. William F. Buckley, Jr.)
Favorite Actress:	Dina Merrill
Favorite Actor:	Cliff Robertson
Favorite Summer Resort:	Southampton
Favorite Winter Resort:	Palm Beach
Favorite Employer:	Christie's or Sotheby's
Favorite TV Show:	"Lifestyles of the Rich and Famous"
Favorite Animal:	The Mink
Favorite Car:	The Limousine
Favorite Club:	Doubles
Favorite Book:	The Catalogue
Favorite Expression:	"You can't be too rich or too thin."
Favorite Card:	American Express

Bonwit's, or to private clubs and restaurants which border Park Avenue. The Park Ranger has never taken a bus, and the closest she's ever come to a subway car is the Paris Metro. Although she is sometimes forced to ride in taxis, she clearly prefers chauffeured limousines and may even have a driver of her very own. She has simply *everything* delivered and calls her doorman by his first name.

The Park Ranger is nocturnal by nature and spends evenings at Doubles, Mortimer's, Le Club, or Le Cirque. She's a member of many committees and attends more benefits *per capita* than any other rich girl. She may even be a benefit queen and support all the diseases. During the daylight hours she reads and shops, for shopping and catalogue reading are the major hobbies of the Park Ranger. She has closets full of designer clothes and is exceptionally well read.

New York is the country's largest city, but for the Park Ranger it's just another small town. She's constantly in the Columns; Suzy and Billy Norwich are probably close friends. She seems to know everyone . . . for her it's truly a very, very small world. After all, she's at home in London, Paris, *and* Milan. The Park Ranger knows scores of society boys and already has plenty of male companionship . . . but I can assure you that she'll welcome a more satisfying and fulfilling relationship. I've known a number of Park Rangers who've embraced poor boys permanently: it can be a warm and very sharing relationship.

$\mathcal{T}$HE $\mathcal{C}$AVE $\mathcal{D}$WELLER

No, she's not a primitive species; far from it, the Cave Dweller represents an advanced state of being a rich girl. Cave Dwellers are descendants of Washington, D.C.'s old and venerable families that settled in the District, or in the nearby states of Virginia and Maryland centuries ago. Although not all Cave Dwellers are rich, it's difficult to live in the same place for generations without saving some money. Personally, I've never met any poor Cave Dwellers.

The Poor Boy's Guide

These prominent families have been called Cave Dwellers for decades, since they insist on keeping to themselves despite the social and diplomatic whirl of Washington. Sure, they attend dinners at the White House, embassy parties, diplomatic receptions, charity balls, and benefits at the Kennedy Center. But while others come and go, the young Cave Dweller and her Mummy and Daddy stay terribly secure in Kalorama, Georgetown, Foxhall, or Chevy Chase. They simply defy change.

Cave Dweller Families

No one knows precisely how many Cave Dwellers have survived until today. Some say it's *the* national secret, while others have suggested that the membership committees at the Sulgrave, Metropolitan, and Chevy Chase clubs provide at least a partial census. Don't worry, however, she's not an endangered species.

As an aide in identifying surviving members of this exclusive species, I've listed below some "correct" Cave Dweller family names. I suggest you cut this list out for your next trip to the nation's capital.

Adams	Key
Addison	King
Ames	Madison
Beall	McLean
Blair	Newbold
Brown	Noyes
Byrd	Randolph
Calvert	Riggs
Clagett	Taft
Corcoran	Townsend
Dent	Train
Fairfax	Van Ness
Grosvenor	

The young Cave Dweller probably attended the Cathedral School before venturing north (Massachusetts) or south (Virginia) to college. If she currently lives away from home, she probably shares a townhouse in Georgetown or its less expensive neighbors of Glover Park or Burleith. She certainly spends most weekends riding and fox-hunting in Middleburg, Upperville, or Warrenton, and enjoys summer days at Rehoboth Beach, Gibson Island, or Annapolis. Her evenings center around dinners at the Metropolitan or dances at the Sulgrave or the Chevy Chase, the social trinity of clubs in every young Cave Dweller's life.

The Cave Dweller has many friends in protocol and the diplomatic corps. She has a keen interest in foreign affairs and knows how to eat with her fingers better than any other rich girl. She plans picnics with Mummy's silver for the Gold Cup, evenings at Wolf Trap, or point-to-points in Upperville or Middleburg.

I've devoted years to cultivating the Cave Dweller and know her intimately; many Cave Dwellers remain my very closest friends. The young Cave Dweller is a remarkable catch and can be quite a capital affair.

The Belle

The Southern Belle is literally from the land of cotton where "ole times" are never, never forgotten. Whether she lives in Atlanta, Charleston, Memphis, or New Orleans, the Belle remains a Rebel at heart. She may be a direct descendant of a Civil War general (the War between the States), a plantation owner, or of families that made fortunes in timber, textiles, or banking.

She's culturally inclined. She's read John Jakes and Margaret Mitchell and is justifiably proud of her Southern literary heritage. She's heard of Eudora Welty, Flannery O'Connor, *and* William Faulkner, but is saving them for next summer. The Belle is musically inclined by nature and loves the classics: she has swooned to tunes by Stephen Foster, danced to the Temptations at hundreds of fraternity parties, and sung "Dixie" at football games from Louisiana to Virginia.

Daddy may be a business tycoon profiting from the booming "new" South, a wealthy banker financing the nation's healthiest economy, or an agricultural baron with hundreds of thousands of acres of rice, cotton, or sorghum. Mummy is probably the first lady of charity and spends endless hours organizing benefits, balls, teas, receptions, and testimonials for civic and cultural institutions, especially the local symphony, ballet, and museum. She's a patron of the arts.

The Belle's favorite schools are in Virginia (Sweet Briar, Hollins, Randolph-Macon, and Mary Baldwin in particular). She sometimes, however, enrolls at Tulane, Duke, or Vanderbilt, or stays closer to home and attends the local state university where she joins the very, very best sorority. The Belle almost always escapes for part of the summer, whether to resorts in the Fertile Crescent or to Sea Island, Linville, the Pass (Pass Christiane), or the Carolina Coast. She's a party girl at heart and even if it's not Mardi Gras or the Cotton Carnival, she's definitely able to find a party somewhere south of the Mason-Dixon line.

For the poor Southern boy (or a Yankee for that matter), the Belle can be a charming and lifelong confederate.

ROYALTY AND NOBILITY (UPWARD NOBILITY)

I know several poor boys and scores of society boys who dream of marrying royalty or their distant cousins, nobility. Marrying royalty or nobility is the supreme achievement of the poor boy. It's a noble pursuit and truly a search for excellence.

The royal or noble rich girl may be called a princess, a duchess, a countess, a baroness, or a lady. Whatever her title, she's likely to be a direct descendant of seventeenth-, eighteenth-, and nine-teenth-century monarchs who accumulated enormous personal fortunes which her family may still enjoy today. Mummy and Daddy may be queen or king, pretenders to the throne, or close

Royal Ruling Houses

The following is a list of the major ruling Houses in Europe. Many of these ruling Houses have sheltered princesses, duchesses, and even queens, whom today even the poorest boy can court:

Belgium	The House of Saxe-Coburg-Gotha
Denmark	The House of Schleswig-Holstein-Sonderburg-Glücksburg
Great Britain	The House of Windsor
Liechtenstein	The House of Liechtenstein
Luxembourg	The House of Nassau
Monaco	The House of Grimaldi
The Netherlands	The House of Nassau
Norway	The House of Schleswig-Holstein-Sonderburg-Glücksburg
Spain	The House of Bourbon
Sweden	The House of Bernadotte

The adventuresome poor boy may want to consider other even more exciting alternatives including the House of Saud (Saudi Arabia), the House of Alasuite (Morocco), and the House of Chakri (Thailand).

relatives with inherited titles and vast estates in Scotland, Andalusia, or the Loire.

The royal rich girl doesn't live in a house; she's a member of a House or even a dynasty which has ruled for hundreds, even thousands of years. A House (see "Royal Ruling Houses" later in this chapter) is an extended family that claims hereditary title to a throne, royal prerogatives, priceless art and jewelry collections, and magnificent castles, châteaux, and palaces. Her family may have its own private preserve for fox or boar hunting, a royal yacht, and a royal flight (aircraft), or a coat of arms.

The royal rich girl may have a very long and very difficult to pronounce last name (try Schleswig-Holstein-Sonderburg-Glücksburg). This is the principal reason that royals go by first name . . . they simply never use their last names. In fact many royal rich girls will call herself "we" rather than "I." It's a polite convention used only in royal society and is called "the royal we."

Fortunately, it's getting easier and easier to meet royalty and nobility. They enjoy traveling, and the U.S. (especially New York, Colorado, and California) is a frequent destination. Although courting a royal rich girl remains a challenging task, it's certainly not an impossible venture (see Appendix C, "The Honor Roll"), so please don't despair. I'm convinced it's the divine right of every poor boy to at least try.

THE OTHER PRINCESS

She may not have a title, but the Other Princess has charms (many of them cast in gold) of her very own. She's not a WASP, of course, and for the poor Jewish (or even the Catholic or Protestant) boy, she's a very special situation definitely worth exploring. She is, after all, a very, very material girl.

Many of my closest friends insist that the Other Princess is *the* authentic rich girl. She does, of course, devote more time to excursions on Rodeo Drive, Madison Avenue, and Chicago's "Magnificent Mile" than any other rich girl: she has a charge account at every conceivable store and is justifiably proud of her most famous discoveries: Gucci and Louis Vuitton. Of course, she is used to being labeled and wears many more labels than the other rich girls . . . they seem to suit her very well.

The Other Princess has never been reluctant to display her wealth and is the ideal situation for the poor boy with a lifelong interest in conspicuous consumption.

Special Situations

CALIFORNIA DREAMING

Whether she's from San Francisco, Los Angeles, San Diego, or even somewhere in between, the California rich girl is truly a special situation. California is, after all, America's most dynamic (if unstable) environment. The rich girl in California, however, is no poorer for having weathered earthquakes, mudslides, the fruitfly, and Jerry Brown. She's a survivor of sorts.

Daddy may be a movie mogul, a business tycoon, or the owner of immense farms, orchards, or vineyards that grow lettuce, avocados, or Pinot Chardonnay. Mummy's probably a famous hostess renowned for her dinner parties all along the coast, an heiress, an award-winning actress, or a leading lady of California society.

The California girl's perpetual tan betrays her frequent visits to Carmel, Newport Beach, Santa Barbara, or La Jolla. She probably frequents the Other Palm and skis at Sun Valley, Vail, or Aspen. She's a natural athlete and is full of energy. She's eaten more kinds of food than any other rich girl and needs to be fed very, very well. She's probably bi—bicoastal that is! She travels to New York for shopping and benefits and frequents Washington for Embassy parties, galas at the Kennedy Center, and White House receptions. After all, Mummy and Daddy certainly know Nancy and Ron.

There are more rich girls in California than in any other state, so please, when the opportunity arises, "Go West, Young Man!"

THE LONE STAR

Whether she lives in River Oaks, Highland Park, Westover Hills, or Alamo Heights, the rich Texan is guaranteed to be a Lone Star in the constellation of rich girls.

Her family tree may include one of the original oil tycoons (a Moncrief, Hunt, Richardson, or Murchison) who made fortunes in the eastern Texas oil fields more than fifty years ago. If so, she

The schools in Texas teach conspicuous consumption—
it's a required course.

probably has at least some of the wildcat left in her. Alternatively, she may be an heiress to a retailing, banking, or real-estate empire that followed the rush for oil, that black gold that's gilded the lives of so many Texans. Whatever the cause of her circumstance may be, Texas Rich is a very, very special kind of rich. They count in hundreds, not tens, of millions. I'm told that even the schools in this state teach conspicuous consumption—it's a required course.

Mummy and Daddy may maintain a "family" home in Tyler or Victoria (the historic seats of Texas aristocracy), or may have a ranch as big as Connecticut and Rhode Island combined. They may belong to the Bayou Club in Houston or the Argyle in San Antonio. If they own land, they probably have their own brand, plan enormous dinner parties called "barbecues," and employ hundreds of "hands."

The Lone Star may have studied at Hockaday, St. Mary's Hall, or the Kinkaid School before enrolling in the "Texas plan": two years at Sweet Briar, Hollins, Randolph Macon, or Mary Baldwin, then home again to the University of Texas.

Special Situations

Although the Lone Star certainly comes out in her hometown, she may also have been a queen, princess, or duchess at the Rose Festival or Fiesta Week. These are statewide versions of the debutante ball, supported by Daddies who belong to the Order of the Rose and the Order of the Alamo. These parties, dinners, and dances (called "coronation ceremonies") last a week or more and

Lone Star Names

There are certain names which are associated with the Texas Rich, that very special kind of rich. While the author can't promise that each and every family listed below has one eligible Lone Star, I can promise you that there's enough wealth for hundreds of poor boys to share.

Albritton	Farb	Moncrief
Alkek	Farish	Moody
Armstrong	Gordon	Mosbacher
Bass	Green	Murchinson
Bentsen	Haggerty	O'Connor
Blaffer	Halbouty	Perot
Bright	Hines	Richardson
Briskoe	Hobby	Schlumberger
Brown	Hunt	Scurlock
Carpenter	Johnson	Shelton
Carter	Keck	Smith
Caruth	Kempner	Stemmons
Clements	Kleberg	Temple
Corrigan	Lay	Thompson
Cox	Levy	Trammell
Crow	McDermott	Zachry
Davis	Mitchell	Zale
Dealey		

are all intoxicating affairs which every poor boy should attend if possible. The dresses alone cost $30,000, $40,000, or $50,000 each. It's the Texan's equivalent to a presentation at court, and I urge every poor boy to get through this receiving line. You may end up with a brand and much, much more of your own.

*E*LIGIBLE *A*GAIN

It does happen . . . even to rich girls. Death, divorce, desertion, separation, and annulment do occur. These, unfortunately, are the unpleasant facts of married life for even the richest of girls. Catholics, of course, love annulments and will spare no expense in buying them. Whatever the cause, however, each of these events may result in property settlements, alimony, and acrimonious lawsuits or simply the acute loneliness of being single once again. Of course, being Eligible Again can be greeted with an enormous (albeit expensive) sigh of relief. Whether it's grief, relief, or a state somewhere in between, this is a very special situation which every poor boy should handle with delicate care.

Chapter Seven

Legends

*S*ome rich girls, whether because of the size of their trusts, the extravagance of their coming out, their legion of security guards, or simply their generosity toward poor boys, have become legendary rich girls. They deserve special mention, together with the serious reader's absolute attention.

As a poor boy who's about to embark on such an important adventure, you simply must be introduced to these legends, for their lives still embody the essential experience of the American rich girl. They not only helped create a civilization built upon the rich girl (whether in Palm Beach, Newport, or the Other Palm), but each also made a dramatic contribution to the rich girl's civilization in her own very special way. Each has made history and has set an example for other rich girls to follow.

What becomes a Legend most is a poor boy with Good Prospects.

The Poor Boy's Guide

Mrs. William "Caroline" Astor, Jr. 1830–1908

Caroline was the wife of William Astor, Jr., an heir to what was then the richest family in America, with a fortune founded on furs (the beaver, not the mink!). William's Daddy was known as the "Landlord of New York" and was the first American real-estate developer: he invented the tenement where many nineteenth-century poor boys and their families lived. William's Daddy left an estate in excess of forty million dollars, all this many years before inheritance taxes.

Caroline was the original American rich girl and established standards that many rich girls and their Mummies continue to follow today. I consider Caroline a true social revolutionary, for she recognized society's incipient social chaos and transformed it into a very ordered social hierarchy—with herself on top. My own experience suggests that many rich girls enjoy this position.

Caroline was American society's greatest social engineer and organized, administered, and controlled its social life during the 1880s and 1890s, whether from her Fifth Avenue mansion (patterned after a Renaissance château) or from her sixty-two room summer cottage in Newport. Her parties inspired the advent of a new kind of conversation which every rich girl and society boy practices today . . . gossip.

Although Caroline didn't invent the ball or dinner party, her annual dance in January and her three-hour dinner parties made dancing and eating French food absolute requirements of being rich. Like many of today's Mummies, she was a devout Episcopalian, made lots of charitable donations, wore diamonds, emeralds, and rubies (many originally designed for Marie Antoinette), and spent lavishly on clothing and decorating (over two million dollars redecorating her summer cottage, Beechwood, alone). She put Newport on the social map.

Legends

BARBARA "BABS" HUTTON 1912–1979

The only child of Franklyn Hutton (brother of E. F. Hutton, cofounder of the brokerage firm that bears his name) and Edna Woolworth (daughter of F. W. Woolworth, founder of Woolworth's), Barbara Hutton defined the term "heiress." She was by any standard a very, very rich girl: when she spoke, absolutely everyone listened. She and her childhood friend, Doris Duke (see "Dee-Dee" following), were frequently characterized by a jealous press corps as "the poor little rich girls." Poor little Babs was worth much more than her weight in gold. By 1924 (at the age of twelve), she had a trust fund that amounted to almost thirty million dollars. By the age fifteen she had her own twenty-six-room duplex apartment in New York and a retinue of servants, while Daddy and a step-Mummy occupied a seventy-room duplex several blocks away, together with a home in Palm Beach, a shooting preserve in South Carolina, and a cottage in Newport, Rhode Island.

Her debut was a historic occasion and was completed in three separate phases: a tea dance for 500 guests at the home of her uncle and aunt, E. F. Hutton and Marjorie Merriweather Post (see "Mrs. Post"); a dinner dance for 500 guests in Central Park; and a formal dance for 1,000 at the Ritz Carlton Hotel on December 21, 1930. She came out in a grand style that has influenced thousands of other debutantes and several society boys.

I'm told that Barbara was a true believer that diamonds are the rich girl's best friend and was an avid catalogue reader: between visits to Tiffany, Van Cleef & Arpels, or Harry Winston, she always had a book (i.e., a catalogue) in her hand.

Babs married many times. Her seven husbands ("the magnificent seven") were typically the beneficiaries of both generous dowries and settlements. I've always considered Babs to be the first truly liberated woman—she believed in the equality of the sexes and sharing the wealth of a rich girl's life. She proved that it is better to give than to receive. She knew how to contribute (especially to a poor boy) and elevated many of her husbands to new and dramatic heights.

DORIS "DEE-DEE" DUKE 1912–

Dee-Dee was the only child of James Buchanan Duke, a nineteenth-century Horatio Alger hero who started his business career with two aging mules and a bag of tobacco, and eventually succeeded in founding the American Tobacco Company and Duke University. At the young age of thirteen, Dee-Dee's father died and left her an inheritance valued at more than $70 million, along with real-estate properties scattered across the country, a private railroad car named "Doris," and a fierce desire to contribute.

Dee-Dee married twice, both times to well-known playboys. She passed on her second husband, Rubi Rubirosa, whose nickname was "Always Ready," to her good friend Barbara Hutton. Unfortunately, he was only ready for Babs for fifty-three days; it was a very short marriage. Like Babs, Dee-Dee was very generous to her husbands and reportedly gave Rubi many wedding presents, including a string of polo ponies and several sports cars. Unfortunately, even her generosity could not save the marriage; Rubi parted company, wealthier and wiser, for he next married Babs. Rubi exemplified the modern axiom, "Marry one rich girl, and you can marry them all!"

I've heard countless stories from aging seniors that Rubi was well endowed with his own *very* private resource with which few boys' can compare. He used his resource constantly (if indiscriminately). I want you to save your resource for the right rich girl.

After these marriages and the unfortunate death of her great friend, the interior decorator Eduardo Tirella, who literally died at the gates of Dee-Dee's Newport mansion, Rough Point (in an accident that occurred while Dee-Dee was driving), she dedicated her life to worthwhile causes and has been actively engaged in managing her own foundation. Dee-Dee lives on a 2,500-acre estate in New Jersey between visits to Rough Point and Shangri La, a home in Hawaii.

GLORIA "LITTLE GLORIA" VANDERBILT 1924–

The only daughter of Reginald Claypoole Vanderbilt and "Big" Gloria (Morgan) Vanderbilt, "Little Gloria" was the center of one of the most famous legal cases of the twentieth century. Her Mummy and Auntie Gertrude (Whitney) battled in and out of court for custody of this young heiress, who at age twelve, upon the death of her Daddy, received a trust fund of $2.5 million and income in excess of $100,000 per annum. In a blow to mother-hood, Little Gloria was made a ward of the court until the age of twenty-one, with her wealthy Aunt (Gertrude left an estate of $78 million in 1946) as protector.

Little Gloria has given
name dropping a new meaning.

The Poor Boy's Guide

Like many rich girls, Little Gloria learned about the value of security guards, detectives, and bodyguards at a very early age. She employed all three to mitigate the very real threat of kidnapping. On visits to her estranged mother, even machine guns were placed at central points in the house, around the estate grounds, and along the private beach. Fortunately, Little Gloria has survived to pursue a career as an actress, author, fashion designer, and Mummy (unfortunately this working Mummy has only sons).

Little Gloria, of course, has given name-dropping a new meaning. She's dropped her own name millions of times . . . on designer jeans, scarves, towels, china, and glassware. She's made Vanderbilt a living legend.

MARGUERITE "PEGGY" GUGGENHEIM 1898–1979

Peggy is universally acclaimed as *the* authentic Other Princess. Her father was Benjamin Guggenheim, one of seven sons of Meyer Guggenheim, a Swiss immigrant who devoted his life to making money. His devotion paid off handsomely, and he established a dynasty built on the precious commodities that every Other Princess enjoys: silver and gold.

However, as is well known, Peggy preferred modern art to collecting extravagant jewelry, Louis XV suites, and mink and sable coats; she spent her time in museums, galleries, and in bed, rather than at Bergdorf Goodman, I. Magnin, and Neiman-Marcus. In fact, she's acknowledged as one of the great patrons of modern art and poor boys. During her lifetime she amassed a stunning collection which the public enjoys today, whether in her villa in Venice or her uncle's museum in New York. Peggy was, above all, philanthropic.

Of course, Peggy left another legacy which every rich girl (whether she's another Princess or not) should strive to emulate. She was addicted to poor (albeit artistic) boys. Her life, like so much art, was both colorful and turbulent, but she managed to have warm and sharing relationships with dozens of poor boys, including painters Yves Tanguy and Max Ernst, and writer Samuel Beckett. She's credited with ending his writer's block once and for all.

MARJORIE MERRIWEATHER POST
1888–1973

Marjorie was the only child of Ella and Charles "C. W." Post, the originator of Postum, Grape Nuts, and Post Toasties and the founder of the Postum Cereal Company. By the age of forty-four, C. W. Post was a millionaire with a successful company and thousands of acres of ranchland in his native Texas (someday to support over 25,000 producing oil wells). Marjorie was to become the owner of the Postum Cereal Company in 1914 at the death of her father. Many poor boys still breakfast on the cereals which C. W. Post's company manufactured: they are a welcome supplement to a steady diet of the rich girl.

Marjorie married four times and would ordinarily have been addressed as Marjorie Close Hutton Davies May . . . but, a simple rich girl at heart, she preferred just "Mrs. Post."

During her lifetime, Marjorie made many contributions to society. She was a great collector of Louis XVI, Fabergé, Sèvres, and almost anything else French. She was renowned as a hostess from Moscow to Washington. She also claimed to own the largest privately owned clipper ship in the world (the *Sea Cloud*), homes in Palm Beach and Washington, and a summer "camp" in New York's Adirondack Mountains. She also knew how to contribute: she gave her Palm Beach home, Mar del Lago, to the U.S. government, and Hillwood, her Washington mansion, to the Smithsonian Institution.

During her lifetime she ruled as the *grande dame* of American society.

The Poor Boy's Guide

CRISTINA ONASSIS 1950–

She's finally put to rest the old adage "beware of Greeks bearing gifts," for this rich girl has the private resources to make even the poorest boy happy. I'm told that she has always demonstrated a generosity to poor boys that her contemporaries should emulate. The only daughter of famed ship owner Aristotle Onassis, she inherited a forty-eight percent interest in his companies upon his death in 1975. Reliable rumor has it that she grew up playing with dolls dressed by Saint Laurent and Dior, and had her own stud farm (she has been married four times) by the age of twelve. She seems to have inherited a "Midas touch" from her father, and she can turn any poor boy's life into a gilded one.

Part Two

Part Two

*How
and Where
to Meet*

Chapter Eight

Sources of Introduction

You have now finished Part One of *The Guide* and should be well acquainted with the rich girl's taste in food, drink, and reading. You've been introduced to her very best friends, the diamond and other gems, and have paid particularly close attention to those events which shape a rich girl's life and distinguish her from her less affluent peers. You're relieved. She's no longer quite the mystery that she once was, is she? You fully appreciate the value of trusts and hope that you'll soon meet a rich girl who's willing to place her confidence and trusts in you. You can't wait to meet Nanny (hopefully she's still alive) and visit Palm Beach and those other retreats which shelter the rich girl during those cold winter months. The perceptive reader knows precisely what to expect from both Mummy and Daddy and is anxious to develop a warm and intimate relationship with each.

The serious reader will want to undertake independent research and review Appendix B, "Recommended Reading," with his local librarian. You may have already subscribed to a number of shelter magazines, especially *House & Garden* and *Architectural Digest*, and you daydream of extended visits to Lake Forest, Locust Valley, and La Jolla. Instead of sheep, you count thoroughbreds at night.

The Poor Boy's Guide

At this point in time, you may feel somewhat intimidated by the rich girl and her very special, at times very exclusive, world. Don't be. In fact, never allow the rich girl's family, trusts, material possessions, or social swim to intimidate you. If they do, you shouldn't be reading *The Guide* at all: you're just not achievement-oriented. Instead you must realize that courting and marrying the right rich girl will be an exciting and rewarding experience. I'm convinced that the poor boy only requires self-confidence, reasonable prospects (see Chapter 13, "Your Prospects"), and *The Guide* to succeed. Remember, your only handicap is being poor. Fortunately for you, the day of the arranged marriage has long since passed. Although rich girls continue to date and marry within their social swim, more and more choose to live happily ever after with boys just like you . . . poor boys. Many of my best friends are classic overachievers—i.e., poor boys who married very, very rich girls—and I know that you can do the same. First, however, you must meet the right rich girl for you.

I have introduced several poor boys to rich girls—often terribly successfully. In fact, my own mailbox is frequently full of en-

It's nearly impossible to avoid rich girls
if you're in the saddle.

gagement announcements and engraved wedding invitations: testimonials to dozens of achievement-oriented poor boys. Courting
the rich girl, however, can become an expensive affair, so please
be prepared. You may want to consult with your local banker or
speak with the scholarship committee. Do you have the requisite
credit cards? You may soon be receiving invitations to elegant
dinner parties, benefits, charity balls, polo games, debutante parties, and weekends in the Fertile Crescent and beyond. Read this
chapter and the four which follow carefully, for they can help
immensely in meeting the right rich girl for you.

There are eight traditional sources of introduction to the rich
girl. Let's examine each briefly:

THE HORSE

The rich girl has had a long and historic association with the
horse. Although the horse won't provide you with a personal
introduction (Mr. Ed notwithstanding), I've always found that
my knowledge of and love of horses facilitates meeting many rich
girls. In fact, it's nearly impossible to avoid rich girls if you're in
the saddle or in the company of a horse or horses. I strongly
recommend that every poor boy become well acquainted with the
horse and frequent horse shows, polo games, and point-to-points
as frequently as possible.

I was very fortunate, since my family's home was within walking
distance of one of the East Coast's most famous hunt clubs. Polo
games and horse shows were literally around the corner—as were
dozens of rich girls. Wherever you live, however, there are many
opportunities to meet the rich girl of your choice through the
horse. The following are a few suggested steps.

STEP 1. Consult Appendix A, "The Poor Boy's Dictionary,"
and study the meaning of the following words: chukker, pinkie,
polo, hot walker, point-to-point, hard hat, trot, and hot-to-
trot.

STEP 2. Read about horses constantly. I suggest subscribing to one of the following publications, which will introduce you to the thoroughbred world:

The Chronicle of the Horse (published weekly)
301 West Washington Street
Middleburg, Virginia 22117

Equus (published monthly)
656 Quince Orchard Road
Gaithersburg, Maryland 20878

Horseplay (published monthly)
11 Park Avenue, P.O. Box 545
Gaithersburg, Maryland 20877
(The title says it all.)

STEP 3. Ask your local stable or hunt club to help you organize a schedule of riding events, including polo games, point-to-points, and horse shows to attend. If you need further assistance, contact either of the following organizations:

American Horse Show Federation
220 East 42nd Street
New York, New York 10017-5806
This organization publishes *Horse Magazine* (monthly) and sanctions horse shows throughout the country. The Federation will be delighted to advise any poor boy of the horse shows nearest you and organize a schedule of show events to attend.

U.S. Polo Association
120 North Mill Street
Lexington, Kentucky 40507
The association publishes *Polo Magazine* (ten times per year) and is the governing body of all the member polo clubs; it also establishes the rules of play. The association welcomes inquiries from any poor boy with a serious interest in the sport.

STEP 4. Purchase a hard hat, riding boots, and britches. Plan an appropriate wardrobe for the polo game and point-to-point.

STEP 5. Take riding lessons. I used to take riding lessons twice a week and found them exhilarating, disciplining, and good exercise. I'm advised by a famous physician that riding develops more muscles than any other sport . . . particularly leg, thigh, and pelvic muscles. These muscles are, of course, particularly important when courting the rich girl. (See Chapter 16, "Sex and the Rich Girl.")

For the serious reader or the poor boy with natural talent and a sufficient allowance or income, I suggest the following additional steps:

STEP 6. Purchase a pinkie and join a hunt club, even as an associate member. The dues may seem expensive, but the investment is well worthwhile.

STEP 7. Play polo. You will need a great many riding lessons (possibly years), but playing polo is a goal all poor boys should enjoy. Don't worry about the ponies yet; if you're lucky, Daddy plays and you can borrow his. Ponies, by the way, are a perfect wedding present from Mummy and Daddy for the groom.

STEP 8. Visit Lexington, Saratoga, Middleburg, and Aiken as frequently as possible. These towns represent the very best of the American horse country, those bucolic enclaves dedicated to the rich girl and her constant companion, the horse.

The horse country warrants your further attention, since it's not only the perfect place to meet rich girls (and society boys) but also because you may find *yourself* a resident of this turf some day. The towns of Lexington, Saratoga, Middleburg, and Aiken each represent special fields of play for the aspiring poor boy.

Lexington, Kentucky: The heart and soul of the blue-grass country, where breeding is a very serious affair . . . it's actually a business and a tax shelter for many a rich Mummy and Daddy. The rolling pastures of emerald blue grass, the miles and miles of white fences, the fabled stables, and the presence of so many thoroughbreds have always given me a profound sense of security.

Lexington: where breeding is a very serious affair.

Saratoga, New York: In August of every year, this legendary retreat in upstate New York attracts scores of blue-blooded rich girls for the annual racing season. Saratoga is very, very social, so come prepared for rounds of breakfasts, brunches, lunches, teas, picnics, cocktail parties, dinners, and supper dances. You'll meet Du Ponts, Mellons, Guests, and Vanderbilts, and dozens of rich girls. As Cornelius Vanderbilt Whitney once said, "Saratoga in August is the most important place to be." It still is!

The Classic Horse Show Events

There are hundreds of horse shows held each year. Although many are strictly local events, others attract rich girls from around the world. The following list contains the names and locations of the most important horse shows held each year. Try and attend the ones closest to you.

Name	*Location*
The Pennsylvania National Horse Show	Harrisburg, Pennsylvania
The Washington International Horse Show	Landover, Maryland
The National Horse Show	New York, New York
The Devon Horse Show & Country Fair	Devon, Pennsylvania
The Palm Beach Classic Horse Show	West Palm Beach, Florida
The Tampa Charity Horse Show	Tampa, Florida
The Hampton Classic	Bridgehampton, L.I., New York
The Ox Ridge Hunt Club Horse Show	Darien, Connecticut
The Lake Placid Horse Show	Lake Placid, New York
The Detroit Hunter/Jumper Horse Show	Bloomfield Hills, Michigan
The Grand National Horse Show	San Francisco, California
The Kansas National Charity Horse Show	Wichita, Kansas
The Upperville Colt & Horse Show	Upperville, Virginia

Middleburg, Virginia: This small village, only an hour's drive from Washington, D.C., has reigned as the undisputed capital of fox hunting for almost two centuries. Neighboring Upperville is the home of one of the oldest horse shows in the country. Both Middleburg and Upperville are bastions of wealthy families from across the country. There is a veritable stable of rich girls trotting, cantering, and galloping over these rolling Virginia hills.

Aiken, South Carolina: This town, not far from the Georgia state line, was designed to accommodate thoroughbreds: some four miles of road in the center of town remain unpaved for the convenience of the many horse owners. Aiken has often been called the winter sports capital of the South and the Newport of the South. Although these claims to fame may be somewhat exaggerated, this town still attracts rich girls from both north and south of the Mason-Dixon line to polo games at Whitney Field, steeplechases, and point-to-points. Aiken is the ideal place to find a thoroughbred of your very own.

Once you're familiar with the horse, you'll find meeting the rich girl so much easier. My favorite example of the poor boy who met the right rich girl through a horse is Captain Mark Phillips. Mark's interest in horses led directly to his meeting, courting, and marrying Princess Anne of the United Kingdom. Mark, who is fondly called "Fog" by his family and close friends, has lived by the motto "the horse is the poor boy's best friend." Several horses were present at Mark and Anne's wedding; it was a beautiful day and quite the romantic occasion.

OTHER RICH GIRLS

You have all heard the expression, "Birds of a feather fly together." Rich girls not only fly together (usually to Palm Beach or the Fertile Crescent), they also prep together, come out together,

Sources of Introduction

Meet one rich girl and you can meet them all—
this is called networking.

work together, and swim together. Meet one rich girl and you can meet them all; this is called *networking*.

A rich girl can be very thoughtful and generous, for these are among her best qualities. If she doesn't have a serious interest in you, I'm sure that she'll have a number of rich friends who will. For, if she likes you, she can make it exceptionally easy for you to meet many other rich girls. I've dated several rich girls who introduced me to absolutely everyone in their swim: other rich girls, rich boys, and, of course, a number of society boys. The *other* rich girl may be the very best source of introduction to the *right* rich girl for you.

THE SOCIETY BOY

Almost all society boys look and act as if they are English—many wish they were. Society boys suffer from an extreme case of Anglophilia. This disease is a function of the society boy's breeding, schooling, and frequent trips to Ascot and Henley. The American upper class has always emulated the British aristocracy, or at least what's left of it. The British upper class, of course, is a vanishing breed: it's definitely an endangered species.

Society boys enjoy cultivating what is called the "Jermyn Street look." This narrow street between Pall Mall and Picadilly houses many of London's most famous haberdashers. Jermyn Street's proximity to the major palaces and men's clubs has resulted in a close association with the British aristocracy—hence its appeal to the society boy. Society boys are keen observers of style and love to "dress up." In public this means wearing tailored suits, velvet dinner jackets, emblemed blazers, ascots, silk fourcade ties, and many, many scarves. (Society boys invented the "layered" look.) In private, "dressing up" frequently means something else, for the society boy sometimes suffers from a terminal case of sexual confusion. Psychiatrists frequently diagnose "dressing up" in private as "the English Disease."

Whatever his private habits may be, the society boy is the frequent companion of the rich girl. He often escorts her to the charity ball or benefit, to opening night at the opera or ballet, or to gala preview parties at museums or galleries. He's an excellent walker. The society boy is the member of at least one swim, belongs to all the right clubs, and is constantly invited for weekends at Palm Beach, the Other Palm, and the Fertile Crescent. The society boy can be a poor boy's best friend and benefactor. If he likes you, he will always be willing to make an introduction. I have a number of close friends who are society boys, and I value their friendship and companionship dearly.

THE BENEFIT COMMITTEE

Rich girls constantly volunteer; this is an inherited trait known in medical circles as a congenital benefit. They appreciate how privileged their lives are and follow the examples established by

Sources of Introduction

Mummy and Daddy by contributing time and money to worthy causes and charities. Contributing is a way of life for most rich girls; it is also, fortunately, tax-deductible.

Although benefits are often held for cultural organizations (the ballet, symphony, or opera), for special causes such as runaways or the homeless, or for strictly local institutions like the museum or boys' club, most benefits are organized *to combat disease*. In

Know Her Disease

Here's a list of the rich girl's favorite diseases. You'll see these names often, so make every effort to remember them together with their symptoms, causes, and cures (if any). Once you're in the swim, you'll be attending dozens of benefits for the diseases and contributing more than you ever dreamed possible.

Disease	Cause
Alzheimer's Disease	Alzheimer's Disease Society
Arthritis	The Arthritis Foundation
Blindness	The American Foundation for the Blind
Cancer	The American Cancer Society
Cerebral Palsy	The United Cerebral Palsy Association
Cystic Fibrosis	The Cystic Fibrosis Foundation
Diabetes	The American Diabetes Association
Epilepsy	The Epilepsy Association
Heart Disease	The American Heart Association
Kidney Disease	The American Kidney Foundation
Leukemia	The Leukemia Society of America
Multiple Sclerosis	The Multiple Sclerosis Society
Parkinson's Disease	The American Parkinson's Disease Association
Tuberculosis	The American Lung Association

fact, rich girls are dedicated to diseases, and almost every rich girl has her very favorite one.

The rich girl is frequently the organizer of a benefit and may be a member of a number of benefit committees which are usually composed of ten to twenty or more rich girls and society boys. The benefit committee chooses an appropriate disease and organizes and plans an evening, with the proceeds from ticket sales and contributions benefiting the disease.

Once an appropriate disease has been chosen, the committee selects a date, a location (usually a hotel or private club), a "theme," and a menu. The committee also contacts one of several well-known musical groups or orchestras, or interviews and auditions lesser-known ensembles, for dancing is frequently required. Seating, however, is often the most demanding aspect of organizing a benefit; this may take hours, even days of compromise and negotiation, for everyone wants the table near the dance floor or the bar, or insists on sitting with members of their own swim.

Organizing a benefit and guaranteeing its success (financial and otherwise) is obviously very exciting and requires endless hours of hard work and planning. An industrious, organized, and dedicated poor boy is always a welcome addition, for there is always more than enough work to do. Joining a benefit committee is an excellent way of getting to know a group of rich girls and society boys quickly and economically.

Of course, becoming a member of a benefit committee is relatively easy to do—a phone call to a member with a well-intentioned excuse, a display of enthusiasm, a contribution, and a knowledge of the diseases is ordinarily enough. Fortunately, you don't have to *have* the disease. The charitable poor boy may want to organize a benefit committee (with a select group of friends) for the disease of his choice. If you're very lucky, you may even discover a new disease; you'll be celebrated and toasted for years to come.

Sources of Introduction

The Columns

Each major metropolitan newspaper has a society column, which is often incorrectly referred to as a "gossip column." The Columns are full of facts, *not* gossip, and they chronicle the major events in a rich girl's life as well as those of Mummy and Daddy, her swim, and her Seniors. The Columns, if read diligently and consistently, can provide the poor boy with up-to-date information on all the upcoming benefits, debutante parties, and charity balls. If you read the Columns, you really don't need a calendar.

I've always found society columnists, although often maligned, to be generous and warm-hearted. They have a very difficult, at times treacherous, job to do; they resolutely work long hours and receive countless invitations, which they often cannot refuse. The society columnists must frequently sacrifice their own personal lives for the benefit of society.

I strongly encourage every poor boy to read the Columns on a daily basis. They are a wealth of information, are educational, and are, of course, often fun to read. The overachiever will want to meet his local columnist, for he or she can be a valuable ally and influential patron. Of course, the local columnist, like the society boy, knows absolutely everyone and can therefore be a constant source of introductions to rich girls and members of their swim.

The Social Register

This thick black book (it is over a thousand pages long) has been a best-seller among rich girls and their families for over a generation. It's published by the Social Register Association and lists the names, addresses (winter and summer), schools, and clubs of literally thousands of rich girls and their Mummies and Daddies. *The Social Register* even includes phone numbers, although you've got to look up your own area codes. It's like a Yellow Pages designed especially for the poor boy.

Good bedtime reading.
All those names are reassuring.

The Social Register provides fascinating reading and is extremely educational. I strongly recommend that every poor boy, whether a college student, young professional, or aging bachelor, add *The Social Register* to his own library. It's simply must reading for every poor boy. I know one society boy who keeps a copy under his pillow . . . he claims that reading *The Register* is better than drinking warm milk for a good night's sleep. Reading all those names *is* reassuring.

The subscription price is seventy dollars per annum (this includes the summer edition and the January Dilatory Domiciles issue). Write directly to the following address to request a copy (please, cash or money orders only): The Social Register Association, 381 Park Avenue South, New York, New York 10016.

Tell them that you're a poor boy and that you read about *The Register* in *The Guide*.

Sources of Introduction

THE SOCIAL SECRETARY

Many very rich Mummies have their own social secretaries. The social secretary assists Mummy in planning and organizing very private dinner parties at home, at the family compound, or on board Daddy's yacht. The social secretary will also answer all of Mummy's correspondence and accept or decline the many invitations that Mummy and Daddy receive. When Mummy decides she wants a party, it's often her social secretary who will decide what to serve, when to have it, and (most important for you) who will attend. The social secretary keeps a lengthy list of appropriate people to invite; she may even have "fact sheets" on eligible men, including several poor boys. Getting on a list or having your very own sheet should be a major goal of every poor boy. Being "listed" or "sheeted" can result in a flurry of invitations to elegant dinner parties and supper dances on Nob Hill, Lake Shore Drive, or Park Avenue, and a chance to meet dozens of rich girls in one evening.

In a few large cities a handful of social secretaries organize and control the social calendar . . . they virtually dictate when and where parties are to be held and who'll be invited. They're social arbiters that every poor boy should know. I suggest that you make every conceivable effort to meet the leading social secretaries in your own city, town, or suburb. I keep a record of every Mummy's social secretary and whenever possible ask to be introduced. The social secretary can be a very powerful ally in any poor boy's pursuit of upward mobility.

SENIORS

Rich girls over the age of forty are called Seniors. Whether they are married or single, many Seniors take a strong personal interest in poor boys. Some Seniors are very generous with their time, money, and favors. How you respond to this interest is entirely up to you. I've known some poor boys who've even married Seniors. It's often a relationship built on trusts.

Whatever the nature of her interest in you, the Senior's maturity does result in a deep appreciation of the poor boy's qualities, especially his modesty, sincerity, and sense of humor. Many Seniors immediately recognize a poor boy with Good Prospects: they know an achiever when they see one. I've known several Seniors who've even taught poor boys to walk. Seniors will have valuable advice and counsel for every poor boy and can be an excellent source of introduction to the right rich girl.

Of course, Seniors know all the diseases (and benefits too) and have been long-standing members of at least one swim or tribe. They are great companions and can be a poor boy's very best friend. I have several friends who are Seniors; I treasure their companionship, their loyalty, and so much more.

Chapter Nine

In the Classroom

*T*he rich girl was sent to school at a very early age. Mummy and Daddy both appreciated the value of an education and were anxious that their little rich girl receive a head start. Of course, Mummy was probably relieved to see her little rich girl enrolled at the earliest age; even with a Nanny or a girl from the Philippines, raising a little rich girl can be a terribly exhausting experience.

Many of the right schools, even at the kindergarten level, required extensive testing and letters of introduction from distinguished family friends and former students. Mummy and Daddy were probably asked for a contribution and were requested to volunteer for a benefit or fund-raising committee. They may even have been required to provide financial statements, since school is terribly expensive and being able to contribute is terribly important. Mummy and Daddy were probably interviewed themselves and may have had to submit references . . . all this to determine how serious they were about finger painting, Mother Goose, and skipping rope.

The Poor Boy's Guide

Of course, Mummy and Daddy may already have been on the Board of Trustees, or there may have been a building named after a deceased family member. In this case, an application and interview were usually waived.

THE PRIVATE SCHOOL

The rich girl, therefore, has spent her very first years of learning at a private school. Every major city and metropolitan area has at least one private school established especially to educate the rich girl. Larger cities may have a dozen or more. At this age the rich girl almost always wears a uniform, which is either blue, gray, or a very muted plaid. Uniforms instill a sense of camaraderie, lessen competition, and cost less than matching outfits from Polo. In private school a rich girl is taught to dress like a poor person but to think and act like a rich one.

Although the rich girl studied reading, writing, and arithmetic, a good portion of each school day was devoted to cultural, artistic, and athletic pursuits. She visited museums, botanical gardens, and wildlife preserves, learned about costumes, sang carols in French, and first heard about field hockey. She also met many other rich girls.

I hope that most of you reading *The Guide* will have no interest in girls of this age—certainly those under sixteen. I love Nabokov too, but let's be practical. You should, however, be well acquainted with at least the *names* of the private schools in your own city or town. Once you're in the swim, you'll be hearing of them constantly, for rich girls love to discuss their schools.

PREP SCHOOL

Most rich girls prep. They attend exclusive boarding (usually called preparatory) schools with other rich girls, and sometimes (but only recently) with rich boys. This is the rich girl's first extended trip away from Mummy, Daddy, and Nanny, and it may be her

In the Classroom

first introduction to society. These schools prepare the rich girl for both college and life in the outside world. Boarding schools are dedicated to transmitting the tradition of the rich girl (and boy) from generation to generation. They are designed to develop character and teach her field hockey, and are partially responsible for the rich girl's many admirable qualities. Attending boarding school also establishes close personal ties with other rich girls and boys, ties which are very important later in life, especially when she comes out and joins her first swim.

These prep schools have a great deal of ivy, long driveways, Greek columns, endless playing fields, and imposing but empty chapels. Most prep schools have classrooms, libraries, dining halls, or dormitories named after famous alumni and deceased Mummies and Daddies. Some rich girls are very, very lucky: they are able to live in a "family" dorm—a building erected by the efforts and donations of a family member. Mummy and Daddy, sisters and brothers, and countless cousins may have lived in this dorm. It's just like living at home: it even has her name outside.

Alternatively, some rich girls who live in smaller cities or suburbs attend country day schools or local schools named after Episcopalian saints. Many rich Catholic girls attend convent schools, especially the Convent of the Sacred Heart. Convent schools are a very special type of parochial school—they were established to educate and indoctrinate rich Catholic girls. The nuns are not called sisters; instead they're addressed as madames. It's here that rich Catholic girls learn how to genuflect, say the rosary, speak French, and dream of poor boys at night.

Finally, some very rich girls attend boarding schools in Europe, especially in Switzerland, where they have an opportunity to circulate with rich European girls (often royalty) and learn how to ride, shop in French and Italian, ski in Gstaad or St. Moritz, and curtsy. It's a marvelous education for the rich girl whose Mummy and Daddy sincerely believe that distance makes the heart grow fonder.

The Poor Boy's Guide

College

Unfortunately, it is increasingly difficult to categorize any college as simply a rich girls' school: the wonderful days of the finishing school appear over. It's a tragedy of sorts. Several reasons account for the decline of the rich girls' school. First, scholarships, financial aid, and student loans have all had their negative impact: even the most exclusive schools have opened their doors to poor girls. It seems that almost every college wants a "balanced" student body; they all want to at least appear egalitarian. Second, rich girls increasingly want both an education and a career, and many take college terribly seriously, at least at times. Some rich girls genuinely want to be intellectual (or pretend they are) and so enroll at Yale, Stanford, or Duke.

Finally, coeducation has opened a number of doors previously closed to the rich girl, and some elect to follow Daddy's footsteps and choose Georgetown, Dartmouth, or even Princeton. Unfortunately, today, rich girls have a much, much wider choice of schools than ever before. Of course, a number of very select girls' schools have admitted men, including many society boys. Vassar pioneered this trend.

In selecting my own college and graduate school, I made a determined effort to be as close as possible to a number of colleges which still by tradition educate the rich girl. Quite frankly, Sweet Briar and Pine Manor were *the* compelling factors in my choice of the University of Virginia and Harvard.

When considering your own choice of college or university, carefully weigh the following four factors:

1. The proximity of the college or university to one of the few remaining rich girls' schools, those very special institutions designed to accommodate and educate the rich girl.
2. If coed, does the college or university have a high rich girl/faculty ratio? Is it a well-endowed college or university (i.e., do many rich girls attend)?

In the Classroom

3. Does the college or university have programs and majors in French, art, and economics?
4. Does the college have a polo team and field-hockey team?

FAVORITE MAJORS

Although rich girls attend a much wider variety of colleges than ever before, most still choose from among a very few majors. Rich girls never major in home economics (they don't *have* to cook and they never sew), geology (they don't discover diamonds, they buy them), or electrical engineering (they're already plugged in). Instead they frequently major in French, art, or economics. When considering your own college courses, you'll want to enroll in at least one French, art, and economics class each. These are required courses for the poor boy with a serious interest in the rich girl. You may even want to major in one of these disciplines. They are the most popular courses of the rich girl and afford the poor college student with a frequent opportunity to meet the right rich girl in the classroom.

French. French has always been the favorite major of rich girls, and it remains so today. Studying French has often been a requirement in private school and prep school, so the rich girl can immediately step to the front of her college class.

More important, tradition and practicality dictate studying French. For centuries rich girls throughout the world have admired the finer elements of French civilization, especially French cuisine, French art and antiques, and, of course, French fashion. After all, what other country has given us champagne, *foie gras*, escargot, the chandelier, Chanel, *and* Saint Laurent? These are remarkable achievements, and the French are evidently proud of them. The French also invented kissing, and rich girls love to kiss (see Chapter 16, "Sex and the Rich Girl"). The French kiss hands and cheeks, and, of course, they discovered and propagated the

113

The French invented kissing,
and rich girls love to kiss.

most intimate of kisses, the French kiss. The American rich girl has inherited this tradition of admiring French civilization.

French is also a very practical language to learn. A working knowledge of French facilitates reading menus, ordering both wine and champagne, and understanding designer labels. French is an enormous advantage when traveling abroad: every concierge speaks French. French was, of course, the universal language of protocol and diplomacy, and at many embassy parties and receptions guests either speak French or use French words and phrases. Finally, speaking French is one of the few remaining signs of good breeding—it's often an immediate signal that you're rich and have been for some time.

Art. Rich girls learn to appreciate art at a very early age. Although Nanny may have taught her how to use crayons and fingerpaints, what really distinguishes the rich girl is that she has lived with art. Mummy and Daddy's duplex on Fifth Avenue, townhouse in

In the Classroom

Georgetown, or estate in Lake Forest, Hillsborough, or Wayzata probably contains several works of art. Mummy and Daddy may even have a collection—i.e., a dozen or more, sometimes hundreds—of Old Masters, French Impressionists, or American landscapes. Of course, some Mummies and Daddies may prefer to collect paintings by artists with very unusual names . . . this is called modern art. They purchase large canvases by artists named Motherwell, Schnabel, de Kooning, and Rauschenberg. They are called Expressionists, Abstract Expressionists, or Neo-Abstract Impressionists. Their art is as unusual as their names and as difficult to understand.

In some instances, Mummy and Daddy may be trustees of the local museum or major contributors or donors. They probably know many dealers and other collectors and are invited to all the major openings and previews. Studying art, therefore, comes naturally to the rich girl and is the perfect preparation for a career in the auction houses, museums, and galleries, or as a decorator.

Economics. Surprised? Well, rich girls are suddenly becoming very serious about being and remaining rich. They've read about the crash of 1929 and the Great Depression in prep school and have probably heard of at least one relative's untimely death during the days following the crash. Mummy and Daddy may have tragic stories about old family friends or distant relatives who lost simply everything; some may have been forced to take drastic action. The rich girl definitely wants to wear her diamonds, keep those dividends coming, and continue to visit Palm Beach; she certainly doesn't want to end as a jumper.

Of course, for the rich girl, economics is not the dismal science. She is, after all, a primary beneficiary of the laws of supply and demand: she's a very precious commodity and very much in demand. She probably maintains a gold standard of her own and certainly believes in the invisible hand.

The Poor Boy's College Guide

The American Guide to College, Barron's Guide to Higher Learning, and *Lisa Birnbach's College Book* are all well intentioned. Two are even well researched and well written. None, however, address the particular concerns of the poor boy wanting to know where rich girls go to college. Whether you're about to select a college to attend, are already enrolled, or are well past the age of learning, you should know which colleges educate the rich girl.

If you're in the midst of choosing a college, this *Poor Boy's College Guide* can assist you in making the proper decision. Whatever your immediate plans for marriage may be, I strongly suggest attending a college which provides ready access to the rich girl. Even if you can't enroll at Pine Manor, Sweet Briar, or Hollins, you certainly can apply to a nearby school. If you're already a student, use this *College Guide* as a reference book: attend mixers, make "road trips," or even transfer to one of those coed institutions of higher learning which have a high rich girl/faculty ratio. For the young professional or aging bachelor, the *College Guide* provides another clue concerning where the right rich girl went to school. You might even consider attending an evening class.

The *College Guide* is not designed to be exhaustive. There are thousands of institutions of higher learning in this country, and I'm sure there is at least one rich girl enrolled in every one. The institutions listed here, however, can certainly claim a higher rich girl/faculty ratio than any other colleges or universities in the nation.

Outstanding

The following three institutions merit national recognition for preserving the rich girl's way of life in an academic setting.

The Poor Boy's College Guide

PINE MANOR COLLEGE
CHESTNUT HILL, MASSACHUSETTS

This small woman's college (total enrollment is 600) is dedicated to the proposition that rich girls deserve a special education, as well as large closets, long vacations, convenient parking, and mixers with the right schools. Once a junior college, Pine Manor added two additional years in 1977. It's still, however, known by its legendary nickname "Pine Mattress." Students here are indeed very friendly, and many poor boys continue to find the right rich girl on this campus.

SWEET BRIAR COLLEGE
SWEET BRIAR, VIRGINIA

This private college for women, nestled near the Blue Ridge Mountains, has been a social sanctuary for rich girls since its founding in 1901. Sweet Briar is a 3,000-acre oasis dedicated to enriching the life of the rich girl. It boasts a fine equestrienne team, the largest private indoor riding ring in the country, and hundreds of stables for the rich girl's horse. It's been a favorite school of Belles, Lone Stars, and rich girls from the North and Midwest for decades. Let's hope nothing changes.

HOLLINS COLLEGE
ROANOKE, VIRGINIA

The impressive Georgian buildings of this small woman's school (total enrollment is 1,000) house scores of rich girls. Nearly half the student body have attended prep or private schools. I'm advised that this school has one of the highest rich girl/faculty ratios in the nation. That's very easy to believe. Although some critics persist in thinking of Hollins as a finishing school, it does have a nationally recognized program in creative writing. No, I didn't attend it.

The Poor Boy's Guide

Hollins has long encouraged visits from poor boys, and there is a small "men's dorm" in which guests can stay for a small fee. It's worth the investment, and I'd advise reserving a room early.

Highly Recommended

These institutions shelter and educate thousands of rich girls each and every year. If it is a coed institution, enroll there and graduate with distinction, knowing many rich girls. If it is a women's college, plan to attend mixers, make "road trips," or even "cross-register." You'll be glad you did.

Vanderbilt University, Nashville, Tennessee. A well-endowed private university: many rich girls.

Southern Methodist University, Dallas, Texas. It looks like a country club. Many rich Lone Stars.

Lake Forest College, Lake Forest, Illinois. The address says it all.

Pepperdine University, Malibu, California. A haven for rich Californians.

Randolph-Macon Woman's College, Lynchburg, Virginia. The preferred choice of many Belles.

Bennington College, Bennington, Vermont. Long considered the most expensive school in the country. Very artistic rich girls.

Vassar College, Poughkeepsie, New York. Coed since 1968. There are some extremely bright and rich girls. Lots of society boys.

Rollins College, Winter Park, Florida. This college has the highest tuition/room-and-board cost of any school in Florida. Many rich girls in session.

Scripps College, Claremont, California. One of only two women's colleges on the West Coast. Definitely worth a visit.

University of Southern California, Los Angeles, California. A legendary party school. Many rich girls in session.

Sarah Lawrence College, Bronxville, New York. For the neurotic rich girl.

Wheaton College, Norton, Massachusetts. The oldest women's college in New England. A social sanctuary for many rich girls.

Recommended

The following institutions maintain a high rich girl/faculty ratio. Write for a catalogue for further information or simply visit the campus and conduct your own census.

Agnes Scott College
Atlanta, Georgia

Bowdoin College
Brunswick, Maine

Brown University
Providence, Rhode Island

Bryn Mawr College
Bryn Mawr, Pennsylvania

Colby College
Waterville, Maine

Colorado College
Colorado Springs, Colorado

Connecticut College
New London, Connecticut

Dartmouth College
Hanover, New Hampshire

Duke University
Durham, North Carolina

Georgetown University
Washington, D.C.

Goucher College
Towson, Maryland

Hamilton College
Clinton, New York

Harvard University
Cambridge, Massachusetts

Manhattanville College
Purchase, New York

Mary Baldwin College
Staunton, Virginia

Middlebury College
Middlebury, Vermont

The Poor Boy's Guide

Mills College
Oakland, California

Mount Holyoke College
South Hadley, Massachusetts

Northwestern University
Evanston, Illinois

Princeton University
Princeton, New Jersey

St. Lawrence University
Canton, New York

Salem College
Winston-Salem,
North Carolina

Skidmore College
Saratoga Springs, New York

Smith College
Northampton, Massachusetts

Stanford University
Stanford, California

Stephens College
Columbia, Missouri

Trinity College
Hartford, Connecticut

Tulane University
New Orleans, Louisiana

University of Denver
Denver, Colorado

University of Miami
Coral Gables, Florida

University of North Carolina
Chapel Hill, North Carolina

University of Texas
Austin, Texas

University of Virginia
Charlottesville, Virginia

Wellesley College
Wellesley, Massachusetts

Williams College
Williams, Massachusetts

Yale University
New Haven, Connecticut

Don't Bother

Rich girls simply *never* attend the following institutions.

The United States Military Academy
West Point, New York

In the Classroom

California Institute of Technology
Pasadena, California

Slippery Rock University
Slippery Rock, Pennsylvania

Rest in Peace

There were three very special schools which were exclusively devoted to the rich girl. They defined the finishing school and were dedicated to transmitting the traditions and civilization of the rich girl from generation to generation. It's with both regret and sorrow that we mark the demise of Finch College, Bennett Junior College, and Briarcliff College.

Polo on Campus

Most polo enthusiasts claim that this sport was first invented in Persia nearly 2,000 years ago and that it soon spread to Arabia, Tibet, China, and finally India, where it was discovered by Europeans. Wherever it was first played, it remains a high-risk sport for both player and pony, one which rich boys and society boys have traditionally enjoyed. Personally, I consider polo a highly refined and sophisticated sport, rather like courting a rich girl. It's also a very good excuse to dress up, picnic, and drink champagne.

Unlike other team sports, however, polo players are known by a number (one, two, three, or four) rather than by a position name (e.g., halfback, fullback). My own experience suggests that many poor boys excel at position number two, sometimes known as the "scrambler" or "hustler." This is a position which requires a keen eye, quick in and out movements, and an aggressive nature. Some poor boys do prefer position number one; he's responsible for receiving passes and scoring. Of course, much of a player's success can be attributed to the talents and movements of his mount.

Polo is experiencing a resurgence on campuses all across America. I advise every poor boy to consider enrolling in a college or university which fields a polo team. Polo can be an elevating experience; as a member of a team, you'll be in a mounted position that few rich girls can fail to notice.

Each of the following schools has a polo club:

Colorado State University
Cornell University
Skidmore College
Stanford University
Texas A & M
Texas Tech
Tulane University
University of California (Davis)
University of Connecticut
University of South Carolina
University of Southern California
University of Virginia
Yale University

Chapter Ten
∽
Choosing a Career

*Y*es, more and more rich girls work. The lingering spirit of the Protestant work ethic, together with the new demands of the women's movement, have made a career increasingly important to the rich girl. Of course, Jacqueline Kennedy Onassis's decision to become a working mother was a watershed event that has profoundly influenced the younger generation of rich girls. She deserves enormous credit for encouraging rich girls to pursue a career and not simply a husband. Jackie, unfortunately, chose not to marry poor boys. We all make mistakes.

Although a job supplements a rich girl's income from Mummy, Daddy, and her trusts, money in itself is not the principal objective. A career permits a rich girl to "circulate" (i.e., meet other rich girls and boys) and to "contribute" (i.e., help society). Circulating and contributing are terribly important to the rich girl. Additionally, a job is always the subject of fascinating conversation at dinner parties, charity events, opening nights, and weekends in the Fertile Crescent, Palm Beach, or the Other Palm; it may, therefore, be viewed as the ultimate form of entertainment.

The Poor Boy's Guide

When choosing your own employment objectives, you will want to carefully consider the following careers, all of which provide ready access to the rich girl. There is nothing easier or more natural than meeting someone, especially the right rich girl, on the job.

BANKING

The financial community and banking in particular hold special appeal for the rich girl. Daddy, an uncle, or a family friend is a director of at least one bank. An introduction is, therefore, easy, and completing an employment application or interview is certainly unnecessary.

The rich girl has spent a good deal of time in her many banks (cashing checks, depositing dividends, reviewing her trusts, or visiting her security box), so she immediately feels comfortable and at home in a bank. The working conditions are excellent, the desks are large, everyone has a telephone, and the hours are acceptable. Of course, bankers can take long lunches, which is especially important during the January and July sales. Banking also provides the rich girl with some valuable experience in managing money—which is very important if anything ever were to happen to Mummy and Daddy.

One bank in particular has always attracted a great number of very rich girls (and boys): the Morgan Bank. It was founded by J. P. Morgan and remains a citadel of power and privilege. Simply everyone seems to have a pedigree or at least a very good story. I've worked at the House of Morgan and can only say that it is overrun with rich girls learning everything about money. I'll be happy to provide any qualified poor boy with a letter of introduction. It's a perfect place to work for a poor boy with an interest in trusts.

Choosing a Career

PUBLISHING

Since rich girls love to read, a career in publishing is a natural choice. A job with the shelter magazines or *Town & Country, Vogue, Vanity Fair, Women's Wear Daily,* and *W* are all highly desired. Many rich girls are employed as assistant editors, researchers, and assistants to assistant art directors at these and other major national publications. Typically, rich girls don't work for *Harper's, The Atlantic, The New Republic,* or *The Partisan Review.* Instead, they prefer those publications with at least a few photos and a somewhat larger circulation.

A few rich girls work for book publishers, where their expertise in antiques, costumes, jewelry, and pictures—and their knowledge of other rich girls—is especially valuable. Jacqueline Kennedy Onassis's choice of book publishing as a career has further popularized this industry.

AUCTION HOUSES / GALLERIES

The auction houses (particularly Sotheby's and Christie's) and art and antiques galleries are traditionally the premier career choices of the rich girl. These institutions pay very little, so poor girls really can't work there. The competition, therefore, is limited.

The rich girl brings several natural advantages to the auction house, or gallery. First, she has a "good eye" and recognizes a good painting, bureau plat desk, or piece of porcelain when she sees one. She knows that Louis XVI, Queen Anne, and George III are not historic figures but things you sit on. She realizes that a Foo Dog is not a snack in the local Chinese restaurant and that Chippendale is a style, not a male strip club. Of course, the auction houses and galleries are full of society boys (they have the very best eyes) and other rich girls. The auction house or gallery is simply the perfect place to circulate.

The Poor Boy's Guide

The Auction Houses

Famous works of art and sculpture, Chippendale furniture, antique gold and jewelry, Oriental rugs, and many other *objets d'art* are sold through the auction houses. Consignments are accepted from all over the world and auctions are held periodically. The auction houses remain a favorite choice of rich girls. If you have at least one good eye, I strongly suggest that you contact one of the following auction houses. They all welcome talented poor boys.

Name	City
Sotheby's	New York, New York
Christie's	New York, New York
William Doyle Galleries	New York, New York
Phillips	New York, New York
Butterfield & Butterfield	San Francisco, California
Leslie Hindman Auctioneers	Chicago, Illinois
Selkirk Galleries	St. Louis, Missouri
Weschler's	Washington, D.C.
Skinner's	Boston, Massachusetts
Robert C. Eldred	East Dennis, Massachusetts
C. G. Sloan	Washington, D.C.

FOUNDATIONS

Foundations were established by very rich Mummies and Daddies, often called philanthropists, to share their wealth (or at least part of it). There are, for instance, Ford, Mellon, Duke, Rockefeller, and Kellogg foundations. Many of the major foundations have particular programs, whether in the arts, social work, or science, which they support through monetary contributions called grants. These programs are designed to improve and elevate society. (No, publication of *The Guide* was not supported by a grant.)

Choosing a Career

*She knows that Louis XVI, Queen Anne,
and George III are not historic figures,
but things you sit on.*

Many rich girls are very familiar with foundations, since certainly one relative or family has their own foundation, and establishing a foundation, museum, hospital wing, or college dormitory is the ultimate goal of almost all rich Mummies and Daddies. This is called an edifice complex in psychiatric circles.

There are several reasons rich girls find a foundation job an appealing career opportunity. Foundations are typically private institutions and are usually quiet and managed like a private club. The rich girl, therefore, feels immediately at home. Foundations are also very generous and have excellent benefits, short hours, and long vacations, so frequent visits to the Fertile Crescent, Palm Beach, and the Other Palm all remain possible. Finally, rich girls simply adore giving money away (especially someone else's) and find working for a foundation the very best way to contribute.

The Foundations

There are over 25,000 foundations, private endowments, and charitable trusts in the United States. Many were established to help assist and elevate society, which naturally includes you, the poor American Boy. It's impossible to mention them all, but what follows is a list of some of the largest in terms of capital resources. I suggest that you write to The Foundation Center, 79 Fifth Avenue, New York, New York 10003 for a more complete list.

Name	*Location*
Ford Foundation	New York, New York
Robert Wood Johnson Foundation	Princeton, New Jersey
Kellogg Foundation	Battle Creek, Michigan
Rockefeller Foundation	New York, New York
Andrew W. Mellon Foundation	New York, New York
Lilly Endowment	Indianapolis, Indiana
Pew Memorial Trust	Philadelphia, Pennsylvania
Kresge Foundation	Troy, Michigan
Charles Stewart Mott Foundation	Flint, Michigan
Duke Endowment	Charlotte, North Carolina
Carnegie Corporation	New York, New York
Richard King Mellon Foundation	Pittsburgh, Pennsylvania
Houston Endowment	Houston, Texas

*D*ECORATING

It would be an impossible task to list all the reasons why rich girls choose decorating as a career . . . there are just too many. Traditionally, however, rich girls have excelled at decorating as Sister (Parish), Chessy (Raynor), Mica (Ertegun), and Virginia (Sherrill) have all shown. Their successes are now being emulated by the younger generation of rich girls.

Choosing a Career

Decorators are, of course, some of Mummy's best friends (they're often the best walkers), so it's very easy to uncover a suitable job while studying for your A.S.I.D. (a qualification from the American Society of Interior Designers).

Rich girls do love to shop (it's another inherited trait), and decorating requires hours and hours of shopping. Decorating also remains the very best excuse for circulating. The client comes first, and you the decorator must visit all the galleries, auction houses, and shops. Rich girls recognize the best sources for fabrics, wallpaper, paints, furniture, antiques, and *objets d'art* from all over the globe. The rich girl knows a *faux* when she sees one.

The only conceivable drawback to this profession for a rich girl is that it's often very difficult to meet an eligible and interested young man. Most male decorators work much too hard to make a lifelong commitment. Many are compulsive: they seem dedicated to spending endless hours pursuing pleasing odds and ends.

BROADCASTING

Since rich girls love to hear themselves talk, enjoy productions of every kind, and instinctively know who and what to direct, broadcasting is a natural career choice. A rich girl may work as an assistant to the producer or director, or in research, video, or film editing, or she may even be a political or foreign correspondent herself. I can assure you that whether it's a job in network news, a local talk show, or "Entertainment Tonight," rich girls are naturals at developing a wide audience. They've had my undivided attention for years.

Of course, Maria Shriver Schwarzenegger's success (albeit short-lived), following that of Phyllis George, has encouraged hundreds of rich girls to pursue careers in every and all aspects of broadcasting. It's a dynamic profession and certainly one well worth considering.

The Poor Boy's Guide

PROTOCOL

The rich girl's admirable personal qualities, together with her instinctive talent for recognizing what's socially correct, contribute to her success in protocol.

Protocol involves meeting and greeting, escorting and entertaining foreign dignitaries, ministers and ambassadors, major cultural and business figures, and visiting heads of state. Protocol requires organizing luncheons and dinners, travel schedules, accommodations, and private social functions for these dignitaries with prominent American businesses, social and cultural leaders, and with Mummy and Daddy. Many corporations, cities, and state governments have recently established protocol departments. The most desired positions, however, exist in Washington. The chief of protocol, who is responsible for hundreds of diplomatic functions and thousands of visiting dignitaries each and every year, lives there. I've known several chiefs of protocol and can confirm that each has needed a great deal of help.

Protocol is a demanding career and a terribly prestigious job, one which requires the peculiar talents of a rich girl: poise, an extensive wardrobe, an outside income, conversational French, and experience in foreign affairs. Protocol is a rapidly expanding profession and can open many doors for the diplomatic poor boy. The U.S. government is the equal-opportunity employer, so I suggest you write directly to Ms. Selwa Roosevelt, Chief of Protocol, U.S. Department of State, 2201 C Street, N.W., Washington, D.C. 20520. Please tell Ambassador Roosevelt you read about protocol in *The Guide*.

MUSEUMS

Some social critics argue that the rich girl is a work of art; others insist that she's a national treasure and part of our American heritage; still others believe she should be preserved for everyone to enjoy. Whatever your own feelings, rich girls often end up in museums, where they work as curators, assistant curators, fund raisers, docents, restorers, program directors, and publicity aides.

The rich girl's family connections on the Board of Trustees, her "good eye" (see "Auction Houses/Galleries," earlier in this chapter), and her major in art history all make the museum a logical choice for a place to work. There are, of course, hundreds of museums, so her choices (and yours) can be very broad, indeed.

The Museums

If you're devoted to the arts, as well as the rich girl, I suggest contacting one of the following museums. Each of these institutions boasts a priceless collection: many rich girls for the aspiring poor boy.

Atlanta	The High Museum of Art
Baltimore	The Baltimore Museum of Art
	Walters Art Gallery
Boston	Boston Athenaeum
	Museum of Fine Arts
Chicago	The Art Institute of Chicago
Dallas	Dallas Museum of Fine Arts
Detroit	The Detroit Institute of Arts
Evanston, Ill.	Terra Museum of American Art
Fort Worth	Amon Carter Museum of Western Art
	Kimbell Art Museum
Hartford	Wadsworth Atheneum
Houston	The Museum of Fine Arts, Houston
Los Angeles	Los Angeles County Museum of Art
Malibu, Calif.	J. Paul Getty Museum
Minneapolis	The Minneapolis Institute of Arts
New Orleans	New Orleans Museum of Art
Philadelphia	Pennsylvania Academy of the Fine Arts
	Philadelphia Museum of Art

Pittsburgh	Museum of Art, Carnegie Institute
New York	Cooper-Hewitt Museum
	The Metropolitan Museum of Art
	The Museum of Modern Art
	The Solomon R. Guggenheim Museum
	The Whitney Museum of American Art
Pasadena, Calif.	Norton Simon Museum
San Francisco	The Fine Arts Museums of San Francisco
Washington, D.C.	Corcoran Gallery of Art
	Dumbarton Oaks Collection
	Freer Gallery of Art
	National Gallery of Art
	National Portrait Gallery
	The Phillips Collection
	Smithsonian Institution

Rich girls never work in factories, on assembly lines, or on oil rigs, although they may own them. Rich girls don't work on farms or ranches, although Mummy and Daddy may own one. Rich girls hate bedpans, needles, and hospitals, so few, if any, rich girls choose nursing as a career. Daddy never lets his rich girl choose an occupation where she may deal with the general public; this is, of course, purely a matter of safety.

In fact, working for Daddy is often the ultimate career objective of the new generation of rich girls. Today's rich girl is often stepping into Daddy's shoes, not Mummy's. The family business does remain a major source of wealth in this country, and more and more rich girls will find themselves the owner of a family enterprise. For the poor boy with enterprise of his own, marrying the right rich girl can often lead to a position as Chairman of the Board. It's the contemporary version of the Horatio Alger tale and a career path on which few poor boys can fail to advance.

Chapter Eleven
❧
The Fertile Crescent

$\mathscr{T}$he summer truly separates the American classes. Don't fool yourself: the U.S., like all countries, has classes; we just lack the class system. Since we don't have a system, entering and exiting our classes is just a great deal easier. That's what makes *The Guide* so important to you, the poor boy, and this adventure in upward mobility all so possible.

If you're a rich girl, you either "summer" somewhere or you stay home. Staying home is a bore, and the rich girl will go to great lengths (she travels almost everywhere) to escape any form of boredom. Boredom is the supreme risk of being rich, but don't worry about that until you're the Great Provider. At this point in time, you still have plenty to do to keep busy.

Rich girls return to their summer nests dependably; it's one of their many inherited traits. The summer remains the very best season to find the right rich girl for you. Several factors account for this. First, the logistics are much easier: rich girls congregate in a few select locations during the summer. Second, everyone looks healthier (the tan) and happier (no school, no work). So, both you (the poor boy) and the rich girl are physically and psychologically more attractive. Third, it is simply much easier to meet the rich girl during the summer months. The days are longer and everyone is outside on the beach, tennis court, yacht club, or marina. All these locations are conducive to an easy (although well-rehearsed) introduction.

Let's first identify the locale for this introduction, for the majority of rich girls gather in a small geographic area. This area extends from Point O'Woods on Fire Island, through the sophisticated resorts of Southampton and Easthampton, and includes Fishers Island, Watch Hill, and Newport. It widens to include the Cape and the Islands (Nantucket and Martha's Vineyard), and narrows again and ends in Northeast Harbor, Maine. *This area is called the Fertile Crescent and is the source of the rich girl's civilization.* For the poor boy, it is also the most fertile territory for discovering and courting the rich girl of his choice.

I've summered in the Fertile Crescent for almost thirty years and (modesty aside) feel well qualified to conduct this important although abbreviated tour. I hope you will soon be enjoying many weekends here and will come to know several of these towns, villages, and islands (and at least one rich girl) intimately. With some luck and *The Guide* to assist you, you will someday have a cottage of your own overlooking the Atlantic, Nantucket Sound, or Narragansett Bay.

Point O'Woods, Fire Island, New York

The Fertile Crescent begins here, a small enclave of only 130 homes resting securely on this long sandbar which poses as an island just sixty miles from Manhattan. Don't confuse Point O'-Woods with its flamboyant (and largely gay) neighbors, the Pines or Cherry Grove, for this summer colony is conspicuously conservative and exceedingly straight. These weathered shingled homes are very deceiving, for many wealthy Mummies and Daddies from around the country claim Point O'Woods as their summer home. The land itself is owned by a private association which rents to home owners on ninety-nine-year leases. Houses here are inherited; they are almost never bought and sold, so if you want to stay longer than a season, you'll have to marry the right rich girl. Point O'Woods is terribly private, and members need keys to get through at least one of its many gates, so please don't go uninvited. Once you are there, however, it's not unlike a rich girl, very warm and welcoming.

The
Fertile
Crescent

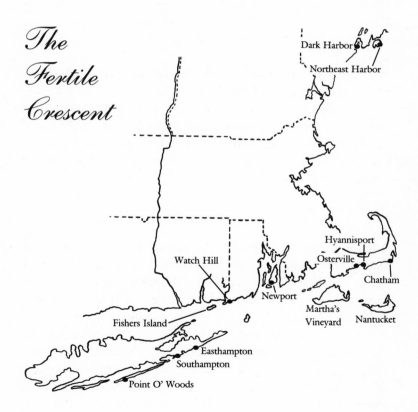

The Poor Boy's Guide

Southampton, New York

This village on Long Island's South Shore defines summer elegance. Its reputation for beachfront mansions and private estates is legendary, and deservedly so. A short drive along First Neck Lane, Dune Road, or Gin Lane can provide the poor boy with a memorable glimpse of the Fertile Crescent. Whether gray shingle, white clapboard, or French château, these magnificent homes with their manicured lawns, pools, tennis courts, and towering hedges have sheltered rich girls for several generations.

At midday absolutely everyone descends on either the Meadow Club (grass tennis courts as far as the eye can see) or the Bathing Corporation (the beach club). It's a veritable safari of rich girls, traveling to their clubs. It's a welcome sight for any poor boy's eyes.

This village is the most socially resonant of summer addresses, and poor boys will find Southampton an overwhelming experience. Southampton, unlike Point O'Woods, is very social. The dance at the Parrish (a museum, not a church) is the highlight of the social season, but there are dozens of private parties every weekend, and a well-dressed and well-tanned poor boy is always a welcome addition.

Easthampton, New York

A few miles east of Southampton (and just a step down the social ladder), this summer resort has been called the most beautiful village in America. Beauty aside, Easthampton has a long history as a refuge for successful artists and writers (Jackson Pollock and Truman Capote lived here) as well as a number of very eligible rich girls. If Easthampton appears much more reserved than its very social neighbor to the west, perhaps it's just the charming village green, the quiet pond, and the classic architecture of many of its stately homes. All this is quite deceiving, however, since Easthampton can provide even the most energetic poor boy with

The Fertile Crescent

an exhausting weekend. The new poor boy in town should head directly to the Maidstone Club, which is the center of much activity, whether golf, tennis, or just a swim on its fabulous beach. I find Easthampton the perfect place to get acquainted with the rhythm of a rich girl's life and to explore her private resources.

FISHERS ISLAND, NEW YORK

This small island (it's only eight miles long) off the Connecticut coast is known as a home of the quiet rich. Although talking is permitted, most residents prefer golf, tennis, or sailing. If invited, you'll probably find yourself spending a great deal of time at the Hay Harbor Club or the Fishers Island Club, so bring your racquets, golf clubs, and boat, and be prepared to use all your muscles.

Some summer residents claim that there are only two ways to arrive at Fishers: by yacht or by marriage. Many poor boys have done the latter, although knowing something about sailing, even if only how to bring in the sail, will certainly help.

WATCH HILL, RHODE ISLAND

This old and genteel village rests on a small spit of land between Little Narragansett Bay and the Atlantic Ocean. Originally developed as a summer colony in the 1840s, Watch Hill has prospered as a small but very exclusive seaside resort. It's often been called a miniature Newport. Although much, much quieter than its stately and very social neighbor to the east, Watch Hill continues to harbor scores of rich girls. They summer in rambling clapboard or shingled colonials with enormous porches or in gigantic Victorian cottages with breathtaking views of the sea and some of New England's finest beaches. During the day, they divide their time between the Watch Hill Yacht Club and the Watch Hill Beach Club. You'll enjoy both.

The Poor Boy's Guide

The rich girls here are usually from very old and very distinguished families—so expect them to be somewhat reserved, at least at first. I've known several, however, who become terribly friendly during a midnight walk on the beach.

NEWPORT, RHODE ISLAND

Newport is the heart and soul of the Fertile Crescent. It has claimed the allegiance of rich girls far longer than any other resort, and every summer rich girls from this country and abroad descend on Newport *en masse*.

Newport was, in fact, a summer colony during the Revolutionary War period, when its climate attracted wealthy families from as far south as South Carolina or Georgia. It was not, however, until the 1890s that Newport became the mecca for rich girls and their Mummies and Daddies. The period between 1890 and 1914, frequently called the Gilded Age, witnessed the construction of opulent seaside cottages patterned after European

A cottage in Newport

140

palaces. During these golden years before the income tax, Mummy (especially Mummies Vanderbilt, Astor, and Belmont) entertained lavishly with extravagant parties for hundreds and even thousands of guests. Although parties are now of a more manageable size, Newport is still exquisitely social and the home of many extremely rich girls. There are even titles here—many of them real.

I've spent many a lazy afternoon at Bailey's Beach (*the* Beach Club) recuperating from elegant dinner parties along Ocean Drive or Bellevue Avenue, the Bachelors' Ball, or from late night dancing at the Candy Shop. Life in Newport is terribly sweet—especially when you're a house guest of a rich girl.

Of course, everything in Newport is done on a grand scale, and *everything* seems to take on an added dimension. After a weekend here, I usually need several days of absolute rest, preferably at Watch Hill or Fishers, before proceeding home. Newport is definitely for the overachiever.

CAPE COD, MASSACHUSETTS

The Pilgrims landed here before settling in Plymouth, and you may want to visit here first before exploring all of the Fertile Crescent. Although the many villages and towns of the Cape originally flourished as farming, fishing, glass-making, or whaling centers, tourism dominates the area today. I've a deep attachment for the Cape, since I spent many summers there as a youth discovering the unique charms of rich girls. Summer residents of the Cape are so accustomed to visitors and house guests that the rich girls here are especially accommodating.

Three towns deserve special mention, for they, more than any others on the Cape, exist as enclaves for the rich girl: the village of Chatham, which lies at the elbow of the Cape; Osterville, with its famous Wianno Yacht Club; and, of course, Hyannisport, the site of the Kennedy Compound. Each of the seaside resorts overlook small harbors where even the poorest boy can drop anchor.

The Poor Boy's Guide

The Islands
(Nantucket and Martha's Vineyard)

These two island outposts of the rich girl boast quaint villages, miles of sparkling beaches, endless marshes, and picturesque harbors. Their physical beauty is overwhelming.

About twenty-five miles from the southern shore of Cape Cod, Nantucket was once a wealthy whaling center. The island was originally settled by the Quakers and still is very peaceful and serene—except during the summer months when rich girls from as far as Texas and California invade its breathtaking beaches and cobblestone streets. The island retains much of its original charm, and the village of Nantucket is full of authentic eighteenth- and nineteenth-century houses that once housed wealthy sea captains. Today, equally authentic rich girls summer in these former captains' houses or in rambling shingled houses overlooking rugged bluffs in Siasconset.

Like Nantucket, Martha's Vineyard is a summer haven for rich girls as well as actors, writers, and celebrities of every sort. Although each of the Vineyard's villages has a distinct character and personality, Edgartown is certainly the island's prettiest town and its most fashionable resort. I've known several poor boys who had an evening which climaxed on Daddy's boat at the Edgartown Yacht Club. It's an experience that makes even the poorest boy appreciate the true value of owning a yacht.

Dark Harbor, Maine

Although the government closed the post office here years ago, Dark Harbor continues to exist as a very quiet enclave for rich girls and their families. Although this island (actually called Islesboro) is only a half-hour's ferry ride from Maine's Lincoln Beach, very few people have ever heard of Dark Harbor, let alone visited this quiet retreat. I feel among the chosen few.

The Fertile Crescent

Dark Harbor is small, and summer residents probably number no more than 1,000; the telephone directory is only several sheets of paper, typically with listings for the main house, the guest house, the boat house, the pool house, and of course . . . the servants' quarters. Only accept an invitation to stay at the first four. I consider Dark Harbor to be the Fertile Crescent's most subdued and most exclusive resort: it's dedicated to inherited money.

Finding a rich girl who summers at Dark Harbor is a very difficult task even with *The Guide*—there are just a special few. Like her summer home, she may be a bit old-fashioned and very reserved, but she's well worth waiting for. I do, however, know at least one poor boy who found the light here . . . he married a very, very rich girl.

Mount Desert Island, Maine

The Fertile Crescent ends here, a dramatic archipelago off Maine's Penobscot Bay that is New England's second largest island. It's a sailor's paradise and perfect for cruising for the right rich girl. It's literally the end of the line for the poor boy, the final destination in your brief, accelerated tour of the Fertile Crescent. Although there are a number of villages and towns on Mount Desert Island (including the once illustrious Bar Harbor), it's the small resort of Northeast Harbor and its neighbor Seal Harbor that deserve the poor boy's undivided attention. The Rockefellers summer here, where the blue blood runs as deep as the water of the neighboring bay.

Although rich girls from Philadelphia's Main Line formerly dominated the summer scene, wealthy families from Washington, Baltimore, New York, and Boston frequent Northeast Harbor in numbers. Daytime activity centers on the Northeast Harbor Tennis Club and the Harbor Club; you'll want to visit both. Everything in Northeast Harbor is deceptively low-key—from the cocktail parties (called "porch breakers"), the cookouts, the dinner parties, and the Saturday and Monday sailing races with their many trophies as prizes. If you're achievement-oriented, you'll want to return home with a trophy of a very, very different kind.

In my opinion, Northeast Harbor is the ultimate port for every poor boy.

Outside the Fertile Crescent

Some rich girls summer outside the Fertile Crescent: they've simply transferred the rich girl's civilization to other locations closer to home. If for some reason you're unable to travel to the Fertile Crescent, head directly to any of the following resorts. Each shelter enough rich girls to occupy at least *one* summer.

SEA ISLAND, GEORGIA

This verdant island is a favorite summer residence of wealthy Southern families and enormously successful executives from around the country. Although the famous Cloister Hotel remains the island's centerpiece, there are now several hundred private villas and cottages which dot the lush landscape. All have at least one guest bedroom.

LINVILLE, NORTH CAROLINA, AND GRANDFATHER MOUNTAIN

Prominent families from Atlanta, Birmingham, Charleston, and Memphis have maintained summer retreats in and around this resort (located near Grandfather Mountain) since the turn of the

☞

century. It's a paradise for golfers, and many mansions line the perpetually green Linville golf course. Linville is a cool oasis for a poor boy seeking links of a different kind.

HARBOR SPRINGS, MICHIGAN

Located on Lake Michigan's little Traverse Bay, this all-American resort is the Midwest's premier summer mecca. It's worth a pilgrimage for any poor boy who wants to worship a rich Ford, Swift, Fisher, or Reynolds in a setting reminiscent of Norman Rockwell.

LAKE TAHOE, CALIFORNIA

Many wealthy Californians have summer (and winter) retreats along the shores of this, the second largest Alpine lake in the world. Whatever the temperature, try and make a visit to test the waters.

PASS CHRISTIANE, MISSISSIPPI

Although seemingly unpretentious, this small town on the Mississippi Sound remains a summer refuge for many wealthy families from the Deep South. The Pass is the ideal escape for a poor boy searching for a wealthy Belle of his very own.

SEVENTEEN MILE DRIVE, CALIFORNIA (PEBBLE BEACH)

This privately owned drive begins outside the village of Carmel and winds past palatial homes which overlook forests of cypress

☞

and pine, golf courses, and the magnificent Pacific Coast. The Monterey Peninsula and this particular enclave and neighboring Pebble Beach have long attracted rich girls. The four-dollar entrance fee is a worthwhile investment for even the poorest of boys.

Santa Barbara, California

This stunning resort city resting on the Pacific Coast is famous for its Mediterranean architecture and alluring beaches. Residents are justifiably proud of the Santa Barbara Mission, the "Queen of Missions," a landmark of California's Spanish heritage. This city, and nearby Montecito and Hope Ranch, remain must destinations for poor boys with a different mission in mind.

Mackinac Island, Michigan

A resort since the 1800s, this small but majestic island remains a summer retreat for wealthy families from Chicago, Detroit, and St. Louis. You'll meet Fields, Armours, Whitneys, Busches, and Pullmans, so please go if invited.

Chapter Twelve

The Flight into Palm Beach

Although rich girls are definitely warm-blooded mammals, they have never been known to hibernate. Instead, when the temperature dips, they display a quality peculiar to migratory birds: they flock south. In some social circles this is recognized as an inherited trait.

During late November, when autumn is reaching a crescendo and the first tentative signs of winter are beginning to appear, many rich girls start planning excursions, perhaps even a season, in the warmer climates of the south. Traditionally, this will involve an extended visit to Mummy and Daddy's winter retreat, or to those of grandparents or close family friends. Of course, a sudden frost or the threat of a brief snow flurry can cause a hasty exodus, extending from Park Avenue to Lake Shore Drive and beyond. I've witnessed dozens of rich girls hurriedly stuff their silk taffeta, tennis whites, Gottex maillots, or bandeau bikinis in Louis Vuitton, Mark Cross, or simple duffle bags, visit one of their many banks, and journey south on the next flight. It's a panic of sorts.

There are, as you can easily imagine, well-established winter migration patterns in which rich girls travel. The state of Florida has remained a principal destination of this flight for nearly a century, and one town in particular, Palm Beach, has maintained the allegiance of the rich girl for decades. The rich can be very loyal, especially to their resorts.

$\mathscr{P}$ALM $\mathscr{B}$EACH

You've already been introduced to Palm Beach in Chapter 5, "Major Events in a Rich Girl's Life." You'll certainly recall that this golden littoral is the *grande dame* of winter resorts and that its social ascendancy began with Henry M. Flagler's magnificent obsession to create a great Florida resort where poor boys could meet rich girls. Fortunately for you and thousands of other poor boys, he succeeded admirably.

In 1883, Flagler broke ground for the Royal Poinciana Hotel, which local historians claim was the largest resort hotel of its day.

Palm Beach: this golden littoral is the grande dame of winter resorts.

The Flight into Palm Beach

Soon Vanderbilts, Whitneys, and Astors were traveling here annually in a social pilgrimage that continues today, for Palm Beach remains a winter playground for rich Mummies and Daddies from around the country. They may be prominent members of society, wealthy entrepreneurs, heirs or heiresses to large family fortunes, or famous celebrities pursuing relative peace and quiet.

Property values on this island reflect its staggering concentration of wealth. In 1984, real-estate magnate Donald Trump purchased the late Marjorie Merriweather Post's seventeen-acre, 118-room beachfront villa for more than twelve million dollars. Although not everyone lives in 118-room mansions, homes here are enormous by any standards, and I've never seen anything which even vaguely resembles public housing. Every house I've ever visited was specifically designed with the visiting poor boy in mind: there are guest rooms, guest suites, guest quarters, guest wings, and even guest houses. One of my closest friends, a society boy of considerable ill repute, claims that staying in guest houses is his principal occupation. He's fully employed.

In my opinion, no other winter resort boasts such a staggering mix of positive features: climate, convenience, social life, security, shopping, and beauty. This potent mix can be intoxicating, even for the soberest of poor boys. It's so very easy to understand why Mummy and Daddy are prepared to spend millions on a pastel mansion, white colonial, or Mediterranean villa overlooking the Atlantic or an aquamarine pool, and why rich girls frequent Palm Beach in such overwhelming numbers.

CLIMATE

I'm advised by local meteorologists that the warming waters of the Gulf Stream pass only three miles offshore and, therefore, make their closest approach to the United States at Palm Beach. This must be manifest destiny of sorts and partially accounts for the endless days of near-tropical sunshine and the inevitable cool breezes that make Palm Beach so alluring. This nearly ideal weather is one reason why rich girls here are prepared to shed their reserve and so much more.

CONVENIENCE

Getting to Palm Beach and staying there is very easy. It's convenient to reach from most major cities in the United States and for many rich girls is only a flight away from her home, Mummy and Daddy's estate, the dorm at prep school, Pine Manor, or Sweet Briar. I'm told that there are more first-class seats available to this city than any other (the airport is actually in West Palm Beach). Of course, once you've landed, life here is simply effortless. Palm Beach has an army of servants, maids, butlers, cooks, caddies, drivers, gardeners, beachboys, and bartenders who are committed to making the rich girl's stay (as well as her guest's) as comfortable as conceivably possible. I've always found staff here particularly warm and welcoming; they seem to know an overachiever when they meet one.

SOCIAL LIFE

The social life here is legendary. During the height of the season there is a marathon of charity balls, benefits, dinners, suppers, luncheons, and dances at private clubs or in Mediterranean mansions on Ocean Boulevard or Lake Trail. There is certainly no shortage of benefits—only of diseases. After consuming several bottles of champagne, a close friend of mine once confessed that "all the good diseases have been discovered—we'll soon have to invent one."

During the daytime, there are endless games of golf, tennis, and croquet at the Everglades Club, the Bath and Tennis Club, or the Palm Beach Country Club, or just hours of serious catalogue reading by the beach or the pool.

The Flight into Palm Beach

For the rich girl, there are also constant introductions to well-known Seniors, infamous society boys, and other rich girls and boys. It's an explosion of socializing that only occurs in Palm Beach and is an easy way to make new and rich friends. I've always found that Palm Beach is the very best place to network.

SHOPPING

Palm Beach has hundreds of small shops, boutiques, galleries, jewelry stores, and branches of national stores, so there are enough retailers to keep even the most acquisitive rich girl temporarily satisfied. Worth Avenue and its connecting "vias" (the Palm Beach version of an alley) have storefronts dedicated to Gucci, Cartier, Van Cleef & Arpels, and Brooks Brothers, among others. This exquisite avenue is the ideal approach for a poor boy hoping to glimpse rich girls doing what they do best: shopping.

SECURITY

The rich girl is always conscious of her own personal security, and Palm Beach is undeniably safe. The four bridges that connect Palm Beach to the mainland all seem well protected, the ubiquitous police department is especially diligent, and the scores of private security guards provide the rich girl with a veritable safety net. The only immediate danger she faces is a surfeit of food and champagne.

THE BEAUTY

Palm Beach's graceful architecture, soaring palms, sparkling cleanliness (money is the best disinfectant), and manicured lawns embraced by clipped hedges, ornate fences, or exotic gardens combine to create an impressive physical beauty that only money (and lots of it) can buy. I've always felt that Palm Beach also conveyed a strange metaphysical beauty that is impossible to ignore: it's an

American landmark to the rich girl. It was designed with her in mind and represents the very essence of her civilization: security, comfort, ease, and luxury. It remains a must destination for the serious reader.

The Other Palm

Nearly a continent away lies the Other Palm, sometimes called Palm Springs or simply the Springs. There is, however, nothing simple about this desert enclave except perhaps the magnificent mountain views, the dry climate, or the pristine air. Every poor boy should visit the Other Palm at least once to really understand what being rich (at least a certain kind of rich) can mean. I've always considered the Other Palm to be like an amusement park for the very well heeled. Although there may be no rides, popcorn, or cotton candy, people here play some incredible games.

Located 107 miles east of Los Angeles and resting below magnificent Mount San Jacinto, this desert playground boasts more Rolls-Royces, swimming pools (over 7,000), and golf carts than any other resort its size. Daddy comes here to play golf with ex-Presidents or Bob Hope. This desert oasis blossomed in the 1950s with the advent of air conditioning, and the population has increased fivefold since then. It's no longer just a resort for retired rich people: it's now a mecca for Hollywood celebrities, famous politicians, business tycoons, and enormously successful entrepreneurs from around the country. Recently more and more rich girls and society boys have discovered its many pleasures.

The rich girl and her Mummy and Daddy may winter in Palm Springs or the neighboring communities of Palm Desert, Indian Creek, La Quinta, or Rancho Mirage. She may even live on one of the very best addresses . . . streets named after Frank Sinatra, Bing Crosby, Danny Kaye, Jack Benny, or Rock Hudson. Residents of the Other Palm are terribly proud of their Hollywood heritage.

The Flight into Palm Beach

The Other Palm: people here play some incredible games.

The season here begins in late October and ends in early May. Winter appears the very best time to visit, and March and April are the very best months for a poor boy to choose a radiant California wildflower.

Hobe Sound (Jupiter Island)

Approximately twenty miles north of Palm Beach lies the narrow barrier island Jupiter Island and what many consider to be the most exclusive winter resort in Florida, Hobe Sound. Although much newer than Palm Beach (the first "winter" residents arrived in the 1930s) and much smaller (there are only about 400 homes), residents are almost exclusively from non-TV dynasties like the Fords, Mellons, Olins, Weyerhaeuser, and Dukes. This small community bordered by the Atlantic Ocean and the Intracoastal Waterway is a winter version of Dark Harbor: very conservative, very understated, and terribly WASP. Most residents join the Jupiter Island Club or the local Presbyterian Church, the two private clubs on the island.

The residents of Hobe Sound are exceptionally security conscious. I'm advised by one winter resident that roadside sensors track all moving traffic and that nonislanders may be requested to register with the police and carry identification cards. I know, it does sound like South Africa, but I've never been requested to register or carry a card; I've always been welcomed with open arms.

Casa de Campo, Dominican Republic

This fashionable resort on the southern coast of the Dominican Republic has suddenly emerged as one of the top international hideaways for rich Mummies and Daddies and their daughters. Casa de Campo is a 7,000-acre compound surrounded by sugar and tobacco fields and offers the poor boy a spectacular vista from which to view the rich girl. During the winter months rich girls from around the world arrive in private aircraft to enjoy its superb athletic facilities, the relaxing waters of the Caribbean, and the casual but elegant social life. I usually stay at the Punta Aguilla, where spectacular villas built by sugar barons hug the coast.

Casa de Campo is very international, and you can easily find yourself conversing in French, Italian, Spanish, German, or Greek . . . or at least trying to. It's the ideal winter resort for a poor boy with a serious interest in foreign affairs.

Polo reigns supreme here, so make sure you've taken at least a few riding lessons. At the equestrian center there are over 1,600 quarterhorses for hire, so meeting the rich girl is terribly easy. In fact, this resort has its own breeding operation, so come well prepared.

The Flight into Palm Beach

Lyford Cay, The Bahamas

Although its 850 members come from over twenty countries, this luxurious private club, located on the western tip of New Providence Island in the Bahamas, has a distinctly British accent. Everyone goes to great lengths to pronounce everything correctly (Cay is pronounced "Key"). It is, after all, on this island that the Duke and Duchess of Windsor once held court. The rich and the famous still visit, and many call this enclave their winter home. The pink walls and white wrought-iron gates of Lyford protect a residential retreat of over 200 private homes with manicured lawns, tennis courts, endless private beaches, and an eighteen-hole golf course.

Most activity centers at the Lyford Cay Club and the nearby Yacht Club. When visiting Lyford, I try and divide my time between both. Although the busiest social season is definitely between Thanksgiving and Easter, you can arrive at any time of the year (day or night) and find a number of rich girls.

Port Antonio, Jamaica

This resort on Jamaica's northern coast is a tropical paradise devoted to carefree yet luxurious living. Originally known as a bustling banana port and a hideaway for Errol Flynn (a former wife lives nearby), Port Antonio now boasts an annual influx of very wealthy visitors.

Although a favorite of Seniors, many rich girls visit their Mummies and Daddies, who own villas at San San or the nearby Blue Lagoon. Some friends of mine insist on spending every February here.

The lifestyle here is deceptively quiet and much more casual than Jamaica's other famous resorts, so you can safely leave at least one black tie at home.

A Place in the Sun

As you can readily understand, all rich girls have at least one winter place in the sun. They're not about to sacrifice that summer tan after so much time and effort reading catalogues in the Fertile Crescent or outside the Crescent. Of course, other rich girls and society boys travel to warmer climates, so if you're going to circulate during the winter months you'll probably have to migrate.

You've already been introduced to Palm Beach, the Other Palm, Hobe Sound, Casa de Campo, Lyford, and Port Antonio. These resorts should keep you busy for at least several winter months. In the event, however, that you travel frequently or receive a flood of invitations, I've listed a number of other resorts which shelter the rich girl during those harsh winter months.

Cat Cay Club, The Bahamas
Balboa Club, Mazatlan, Mexico
Mill Reef Club, Antigua
Round Hill, Jamaica
Tryall Golf and Beach Club, Jamaica
Naples, Florida
Palm Club, Miami, Florida
The Mid Ocean Club, Bermuda

On the Slopes

With the cost of transportation, lift tickets, equipment, ski outfits, and lodging and meals (not to mention the expenses of the *après-ski* scene), it's difficult to imagine that there is anyone poor left on the nation's ski slopes and trails. Whether it's on the slopes, in the lodge, or at a private party at Mummy and Daddy's chalet, cabin, or condominium, the ski vacation can provide the perfect setting for meeting the right rich girl for you. Personally, I've always found that my own skis parallel those of scores of rich girls on the nation's ski slopes. I've always been willing to break trail and head in the direction of an eligible rich girl and hope you'll be prepared to do the same.

Rich girls discovered the many pleasures of this sport years ago, and many devote at least a week or two every winter to skiing, or at least *après* skiing (drinking champagne and dancing till dawn). Many rich girls have, in fact, developed a passion for skiing that they are ready and willing to share with the right poor boy. Sharing the chair lift can be the very first step in a truly elevating experience . . .

Many poor boys have enjoyed traversing steep inclines, moguls (mounds of hard snow, *not* Daddies), summits, and a full range of terrains in the company of a rich girl. A few have been fortunate enough to experience the ultimate pleasure of deep, deep powder . . . there's nothing I know which can compare with plunging into virgin snow. Sure, it's a struggle at first, but once your muscles relax, it's technique more than strength that will count. It's an indulgence all poor boys should enjoy: it's the ultimate physical experience.

I'm convinced that skiing is just as much an exercise in mental discipline as a physical sport. To be a true success, you should always be thinking about what you'll be doing next. It requires practice, technique, appropriate clothes, good equipment, mental discipline, and some natural ability. It's not unlike courting the rich girl. In fact, many of the lessons you learn on the ski slope (whether positioning the pole, your stance, or simply your downward motion) can easily be applied to the right rich girl.

Since skiing conveys so many important lessons as well as providing an opportunity to meet the right rich girl, it's important that you're very familiar with at least some of the nation's most important slopes. I know that three in particular are terribly significant, since they attract an avalanche of rich girls each and every year.

The Poor Boy's Guide

Aspen, Colorado

During the late 1880s, Aspen's seven great silver mines made it a booming mining town. Recently, this mountain resort has emerged as a gold mine for poor boys engaged in a different kind of pursuit, for Aspen attracts rich girls from both coasts. It's also a favorite of wealthy Lone Stars. Mummy and Daddy may have a lodge in Starwood, a ski house in Aspen, or a condominium with Jacuzzis or saunas at Snowmass.

Aspen remains the largest of the ski resorts in the U.S. It actually consists of four mountains and two towns, each with its own special style and character. All, however, share the same natural resources (snow and rich girls), and whether it's Aspen Mountain, Buttermilk, Snowmass, or Aspen Highlands, this skiing center can accommodate the novice, the bold intermediate, or the truly expert poor boy. My favorite run is Jackpot, on Aspen Mountain; it's definitely a blend of trail and tree skiing, and certainly not for the novice. Of course, Jackpot was designed especially with the poor boy in mind.

Sun Valley, Idaho

This resort was founded by Averell Harriman in 1935 because he had tired of traveling to Switzerland, France, and Austria to ski. What began simply as a matter of convenience quickly developed into a winter hideaway for celebrities (Ingrid Bergman, Clark Gable, and Gary Cooper all owned homes here), and Sun Valley remains a primary skiing destination for many rich girls.

This fashionable ski resort actually encompasses Sun Valley, Warm Springs, Elkhorn Village, and the town of Ketchum, once the largest sheep- and lamb-shipping station in the nation. Personally, I prefer staying at the Sun Valley Lodge or at one of the many private homes nearby. Although Sun Valley is particularly popular with rich Californians, there are always a number of eligible rich girls from across the country. The list of owners of houses, cabins, and condominiums at this resort reads like a page from *Who's Who* of famous and wealthy Americans.

Sun Valley boasted the first chair lift, which was invented by Harriman's railroad engineers in 1936. It has carried poor boys to heights that they never, in their wildest imagination, expected to experience. Many experts insist that Sun Valley has some of the best-groomed trails and the finest cross-country terrain in the United States. My favorite runs are on Dollar Mountain . . . for obvious reasons. Every poor boy should test his skills there before breaking trail in a direction of his own choice.

VAIL, COLORADO

This resort, 110 miles west of Denver, opened in 1962 with one lodge and a few ski trails. It certainly ranks as one of skiing's great boom towns and has grown tremendously since then. It now sports a wealth of runs and enough rich girls to keep hundreds of poor boys satisfied. It's certainly the most expensive ski resort in Colorado and prides itself on accommodating the very rich in cabins, condominiums, and lodges spread across the mountainside or in the village of Vail itself. I've always found the rich girls here equally accommodating; they seem determined to satisfy almost every need. Of course, the *après-ski* scene here can only be described as frenetic . . . everyone seems anxious to get out of their Nordicas, Langes, or Dalaboots.

Vail has over sixty miles of slopes and trails, so there's a tremendous amount of exploring which is possible. If you have no luck here, however, try nearby Beaver Creek, a newer development with spectacular private homes and rows of luxury condominiums.

Other Slopes of Note

Stowe, Vermont
Jackson Hole, Wyoming
Taos, New Mexico
Deer Valley, Utah
Snowbird, Utah
Gstaad, Switzerland
San Moritz, Switzerland
Squaw Valley, California

The Country Club

Like the Fertile Crescent, the country club is an indispensable part of the rich girl's civilization. It's here that she learned how to swim and play tennis, golf, and paddleball. When not visiting Mummy and Daddy's cottage at Newport, Sea Island, or Harbor Springs, she'll use at least some of the club's many facilities. Of course, she's been to many engagement parties, wedding receptions, debuts, and other celebrations at the club. It's certainly been a focal point of her life.

Although there are nearly 5,000 country clubs in the U.S., only a few are dedicated exclusively to the rich girl. Listed below are only those few clubs I've had a chance to visit in my own very serious pursuit of the rich girl.

☞

Club	Location
The Country Club	Brookline, Massachusetts
Apawamis Club	Westchester County, New York
Country Club of Detroit	Grosse Pointe Farms, Michigan
River Oaks Country Club	Houston, Texas
Los Angeles Country Club	Los Angeles, California
Burlingame Country Club	Hillsborough, California
Brook Hollow Golf Club	Dallas, Texas
La Jolla Country Club	La Jolla, California
Onwentsia Country Club	Lake Forest, Illinois
Woodhill Country Club	Wayzata, Minnesota
Philadelphia Country Club	Gladwyne, Pennsylvania
Allegheny Country Club	Sewickley, Pennsylvania
Baltimore Country Club	Baltimore, Maryland
Chevy Chase Country Club	Chevy Chase, Maryland
Woodmont Country Club	Rockville, Maryland
River Crest Country Club	Fort Worth, Texas
The Piedmont Driving Club	Atlanta, Georgia
Morris Country Club	Convent Station, New Jersey
Everglades Club	Palm Beach, Florida
Piping Rock Club	Locust Valley, New York
Maidstone Club	East Hampton, New York
Shinnecock Hills Golf Club	Southampton, New York
Quail Hollow Country Club	Charlotte, North Carolina
Country Club of Westchester	Westchester County, New York
Waverly Country Club	Portland, Oregon
Memphis Country Club	Memphis, Tennessee
Kansas City Country Club	Kansas City, Kansas
Hillcrest Country Club	Los Angeles, California
Century Country Club	White Plains, New York
The Country Club of Virginia	Richmond, Virginia
Indian Hills Country Club	Winnetka, Illinois
Oklahoma City Country Club	Oklahoma City, Oklahoma

Part Three

❦

The Courtship

Chapter Thirteen
Your Prospects

$\mathcal{Y}$ou think you're becoming an authority rather easily, don't you? Well, remember, a little knowledge, especially about the rich girl, can often be a very dangerous thing, so please proceed cautiously at first. We don't want anything or anyone to jeopardize the outcome of this profitable and rewarding adventure. We certainly don't want you to repeat needlessly any unfortunate miscalculations or costly mistakes that have plagued other poor boys. (See Appendix B, "Recommended Reading," for *An American Tragedy.*) Although I'm certainly committed to your ultimate success, even I can't tolerate or condone criminal behavior. This is, after all, fundamentally a romantic endeavor.

Let's pause for just a moment and review your progress to date—it should be very encouraging.

You've now finished Part One and Part Two of *The Guide,* and I am sure that your initial intimidation has vanished and that you are well on your way to understanding the rich girl and penetrating the mystery. You've come to recognize her immediately, whether on the street, in the classroom, or on the job. You've mastered the art of introduction and are comfortable in every conceivable social situation. With proper planning, a positive attitude, and some luck, you'll soon be sharing the wealth of a rich girl's life.

At this point in time, your primary objective remains meeting as many rich girls as physically possible. Never let up, no matter how exhausting the challenge may appear at first. Set a goal of meeting at least one rich girl every week and try for two on weekends. You'll find it so much easier than you think! When you do meet a rich girl, reward yourself for a job well done: buy something you'll use later in life, perhaps a pair of opera slippers, a new edition of the *Social Register,* a champagne cooler, or a hard hat. This is what I call positive reinforcement . . . it will make you feel good about yourself and your very special goal.

I strongly suggest that every reader keep both a diary and a very private black book listing every rich girl whom you meet (and her vital statistics). *The Poor Boy's Little Black Book* should contain all those names, addresses, and phone numbers that every boy, rich or poor, desperately wants. Never rely on your memory. Write absolutely everything down, for courting the rich girl is just too important a proposition for any possible error.

My own little black book contains literally hundreds of entries. It's priceless, and even Lloyd's won't insure it. I've had outrageous offers from dozens of society boys, all of whom desired a peek at my book. I've always politely but firmly declined, and advise you to do the very same. I do hope that you'll find the entry on the next page from my own little black book helpful in organizing your very own.

I keep my own little black book in a safe but very convenient place (no, I'm not going to tell you where). I never leave home without it.

Before courting the rich girl of your choice in earnest, however, you must recognize the absolute necessity of having good Prospects and communicating them effectively. Although your Prospects will never be mentioned directly, they will constantly be considered by the rich girl, her Mummy and Daddy, and her swim. Good Prospects are terribly important: in fact, they are

The Poor Boy's
Little Black Book

Last Name:	Whitney
First Name:	Barbara
Nickname:	Buffy
Addresses:	Lake Shore Drive East, Chicago, Illinois
	"Ocean View," Newport, Rhode Island
	(Summer)
	14 Lake Trail, Palm Beach, Florida
	(Winter)
Phone #:	(312) 732-8512 (Chicago)
Daddy:	Robert Whitney V
Daddy's Job:	Private Investor
Mummy:	Consuelo
Mummy's Interests:	Cancer, Louis XVI, Impressionist Art
Prep School:	Foxcroft
College:	Rollins (2 years), University of Denver
	(B.A.)
Favorite Foods:	Oysters, Artichokes, and Häagen-Dazs
	(together)
Pleasures:	Drinking Champagne for Breakfast,
	Skinny-Dipping
Her Vital Statistics:	
Trust Funds:	Yes (at least two)
Estimated Worth:	Mummy and Daddy appear in *Forbes*
	(under "Great Family Fortunes")
Present Value:	$50 million—not including Van Goghs
	and Renoirs
Future Value:	Can't calculate accurately; depends on
	the art market
Annual Income:	More than mine
Heiress:	Yes __X__ No _____

critical if you're to learn to swim, pursue a serious courtship, and make a successful proposal.

Your Prospects convey more than how you will succeed monetarily, for frankly, with a successful proposal, money (at least earning it) will no longer be an issue. Instead, your Prospects suggest a great deal about your future as a spouse, a Daddy, and a member of society (whether in a swim or later in life as a member of a tribe). Clearly, your Prospects, or lack thereof, can either make or break you. Unfortunately, I've known a few poor boys who never attempted to develop or communicate their Prospects. The results were tragic. They never got to make a proposal—they didn't even get to swim.

I've always believed that Jay Gatsby's great failure was one of communication. He should have taken lessons from the Great Communicator. He had the classic refrigerator, great champagne, a wardrobe, and much, much more. But Daisy (her marriage aside) still spurned his subtle advances. Jay was a poor communicator and suffered terribly for this shortcoming. If your Prospects are good, however, and if you can communicate them effectively, I can guarantee the success of this adventure. So before proceeding with a serious courtship, the Chain of Giving, the Perfect Date, and Sex with the Rich Girl, let's carefully examine your prospects and learn how to improve and communicate them.

Your Refrigerator

Since food is so integral to a rich girl's life, it's critical that the poor boy display an appreciation for fine food and keep a well-stocked refrigerator. An empty refrigerator is a very, very bad sign. Remember, the rich girl is an avid eater: she wants someone who will feed her and feed her well. (For some rich girls, eating well is the only revenge.) I strongly suggest that every poor boy make a determined effort to develop a close personal relationship

The Classic Refrigerator

No matter what you prefer to eat, the rich girl's diet reflects her advanced state of taste. Every poor boy should attempt to develop and maintain a classic refrigerator, one that contains at least a modest supply of all the foods a rich girl will ever need or want. Of course, there are some things a rich girl will never eat . . . but you'll find that out soon enough. Remember, you always want her to leave satisfied.

Here's a poor boy's grocery list.

Truffles	(for just about everything)
Blue Point Oysters	(two dozen, constantly iced and chilled)
Smoked Salmon	(enough for a midnight snack for two)
Caviar	(at least two 16-oz. jars of Beluga—one for the evening, another for breakfast)
Pâté	(preferably *foie gras*—make sure it's fresh *and* French)
Cold Lobster, Crab, or Shrimp	(great any time of day)
Hot Sauce	(for the cold lobster, crab, or shrimp)
Any Type of Finger Food	(an assortment of canapés will do)
Onions	(for the caviar and salmon)
Prosciutto	(for the melons)
Melons	(for the prosciutto)
Watercress	(for every plate)
Ice Cream/Sorbet	(Only Italian gelato and only French sorbet)
Lots of Fresh Fruit	(anything exotic and with lots of seeds—especially mango, kiwi, pomegranate)
Chilled Champagne	(several magnums)
Diet Soda	(a variety of classic diet drinks)
Mineral Water	(only Saratoga, *no* substitutes)

with the proprietor of the nearest delicacy shop. I've discovered the true value of friendship when I suddenly needed smoked salmon, caviar, or a special *pâté* for an unexpected rich visitor.

The Classic Refrigerator.

ℽour ℳallet

Rich girls don't come cheap. Although the rich girl is clearly not about to judge you on the size of your wallet (or anything else for that matter), she may expect many perfect dates and a variety of presents before submitting to your advances. Courting the rich girl can be a very expensive proposition, given her advanced state of taste in food, drink, clothing, and jewelry. Nor can you expect to fly to the Fertile Crescent, Palm Beach, or the Other Palm for free.

Your Prospects

Every poor boy must, therefore, have sufficient financial resources to undertake this endeavor and to court properly the rich girl of his choice. The money which you spend is not just "money well spent"; it's a down payment on your future. It's an investment with nearly an infinite rate of return. It's the first big step in sharing the wealth of a rich girl's life.

If you're still in college or graduate school, I strongly advise approaching the scholarship committee or the student aid society. I'm sure you'll get a sympathetic hearing. You might even promise them a dormitory, library, or donation to the art collection if you're successful. If necessary you may want to show them a few pages from your own little black book. I'm sure they'll be impressed. If you're a young professional, meet your local banker and arrange for a line of credit. Give him a copy of *The Guide* and he'll certainly understand. Whatever your financial status may be, make sure that you have enough credit cards; certainly have all the majors, including Diners Club, Visa, MasterCard, and American Express.

Your Feet

A rich girl will expect you to be quick on your feet. She appreciates a good dancer, and many a poor boy has danced his way into a rich girl's heart (as well as her cottage in Newport, the ski lodge at Vail, and the stables in Lexington). Almost every benefit, ball, debut, and charity event you attend will require hours of dancing with the rich girl, members of her swim, Mummy, or other prominent Seniors. Dancing is like death and taxes: you can't avoid it, so learn to enjoy it. Take lessons if you must.

Since rich girls love to dance, the poor boy who's quick on his feet has a natural advantage: he's free to circulate quickly and quietly. Dancing is simply one of the best ways to network, and a good dancer is always in demand. Of course, society boys dance as fast as they can: they're incredibly adept at twisting and turning at inconceivable angles. They've had so much practice.

The Poor Boy's Guide

Your Ears

Have your hearing checked. Rich girls love to talk and expect their dates to be good listeners. The rich girl, in fact, can talk about almost anything and probably will. She'll almost certainly discuss her favorite foods, books, designers, decorators, jewelry and other rich girls, so be prepared for many long and interesting conversations. Of course, she'll also have endless and often complicated stories about Nanny, prep school, her coming out, trips to Europe, and Mummy and Daddy. Be patient, listen well, and learn as much as you possibly can. It may all sound unfamiliar at first, but soon you'll be sharing the wealth and the talking.

Your Interests

The rich girl is prepared to share her life and her wealth, provided that you share at least a few of her many interests. I'm convinced that the poor boy must take a serious interest in the diseases, good food, French champagne, art and antiques, sailing, *haute couture,* and those other interests which fill a rich girl's days and nights. I've known several poor boys who've enrolled in courses, subscribed to specialized periodicals (especially catalogues, *Antiques,* and *The New England Journal of Medicine*), or did independent research of their own. The more you can talk about these subjects with the rich girl, her Mummy and Daddy, and her swim, the better your Prospects are.

Your Job

Rich girls rarely marry the permanently unemployed. If you're out of the classroom, some form of reasonable employment is required or should at least be anticipated in the near future. Reasonable employment includes any of those occupations listed in Chapter 10, "Choosing a Career," but also includes medicine, law, real estate, and diplomacy. Rich girls rarely marry mailmen, nurses, gas-station attendants, truck drivers, or longshoremen, although I know several rich girls who would benefit from a serious relationship with any of these.

YOUR WARDROBE

A poor boy's wardrobe is one of the most important factors which determines his success with the rich girl of his choice. Although clothes may no longer make the man, they certainly can make a poor boy. A well-dressed poor boy can display confidence and a presence which is simply impossible to ignore. Therefore, whether you're in college, graduate school, or on the job, a well-planned wardrobe is critical if you're to convey the correct Prospects. Whether it's casual or formal, your attire says a great deal about you . . . it literally speaks for and about you.

First, you must also learn to exercise judgment and taste in purchasing and wearing clothing. Never wear anything too tight or clothes which aren't made from natural fibers. Never wear anything which shines and only wear black at night. Only wear leather on Mummy and Daddy's ranch or when riding. Only society boys wear leather pants, and that's hours after the Palm Beach Ball.

I learned the importance and value of a wardrobe at a very early age. This required endless hours at Chipp, J. Press, and Brooks Brothers, but it is never too late for even the poorest of boys to learn. I'll give you some valuable advice and help.

The Poor Boy's Wardrobe

I assume that every poor boy has clean underwear, socks, several cotton button-down shirts, a few suits (no polyester, please), at least a dozen Shetland sweaters, shoes, and an umbrella and a raincoat. This is a "survival" wardrobe that even the poorest boy needs. Without these clothes you can't even get near a rich girl . . . you can't claim to be dressed at all.

The serious reader must be prepared to invest in his future and purchase a wardrobe appropriate to this noble pursuit. I suggest that you bring the following list to Paul Stuart, Brooks Brothers, Louis, Britches, Capper & Capper, or whatever men's store you choose and start with the correct wardrobe now.

One black tie (shawl collar)	Riding boots
One blue blazer	One pair white ducks (for Daddy's yacht)
One pair Bermuda shorts	Something Madras (make sure it bleeds)
Several pairs of tennis shorts (whites only)	Something green
Several polo shirts	Something pink
One Lily Pulitzer bathing suit (for Bailey's Beach)	Several pairs of loafers
One pair of sailing shorts	One pair of Topsiders
Riding britches	Several silk ties

The overachiever or the poor boy with extra spending money (or a very good credit line) will want to consider the following items. If you have all these, you can dress like a society boy but act like a poor boy. That's quite an accomplishment.

A second black tie (peak collar)	Several ascots

Your Prospects

A white tie	Opera slippers
A pinkie	A signet ring (wear it on your pinkie, the finger not the coat)
A Chesterfield coat (get the velvet collar)	One pair of patent-leather pumps
A cashmere coat	

Your Character

The rich girl wants a man of character. Her Nanny, private school, prep school, and perhaps even college were all designed to build and instill character. Mummy and Daddy have character, and the rich girl will want you to have character too.

She expects and deserves honesty (at least sometimes), certainly wants your respect (all the time) and courtesy (constantly). She admires generosity (she wants you to contribute), kindness, and thoughtfulness (she loves presents). Of course the rich girl demands infinite patience and a well-developed sense of humor.

Your Time

The rich girl will demand a great deal of your time; she'll want you as an escort, a traveling companion, a dinner date, a dancing partner and (hopefully) a lifelong mate. She may be looking for a poor boy for all seasons, whether it's Saratoga in August, the Fertile Crescent in June or July, Palm Beach in December, or the spring in Lexington.

I've always found that the rich girl merits my undivided time and attention. I'm sure you'll feel precisely the same.

Chapter Fourteen
The Perfect Date

$\mathscr{I}$ know that you're anxious to get started . . . you've been waiting far too long for this all to happen. Let's be patient, however, and relax just a few minutes before going on your very first date with a rich girl. The best things in life are worth waiting for, and that certainly includes the right rich girl.

You have decided that you'll soon have to focus your attentions on one, two, or three rich girls . . . whatever your social calendar permits and your checkbook can possibly afford. Although you certainly should meet as many rich girls as possible (keep filling those pages in *The Poor Boy's Little Black Book*), I strongly recommend that you concentrate your efforts on **one** rich girl at a time. Husband your energies for the right rich girl.

I strongly suggest that you consider carefully your own emotional, physical, and material needs, measure each rich girl you meet quickly and economically, and make a choice as soon as you reasonably can. You don't want to dissipate any of your valuable (perhaps limited) resources on a "shotgun approach." Instead, you want to aim for a very special rich girl who can satisfy all your needs. With some luck, this will be the right rich girl for you.

The Perfect Date

Courtship requires a personal commitment to one very special rich girl. It is a valuable and worthwhile tradition composed of many days and evenings together, presents, and sex with the rich girl. Courting the rich girl is a romantic interlude that only a few poor boys will ever experience. Enjoy it. For after a successful proposal, an engagement, and marriage to the right rich girl, you must face the burden and realities of the life of the rich: never-ending problems with the staff, constant meetings with lawyers, accountants, and bankers, frequent requests for donations and contributions, and the all-consuming social obligations that only the rich are forced to bear. They really do need their retreats in Hobe Sound, Newport, or Pebble Beach.

Before you go on a perfect date, commence the Chain of Giving, and have sex with the rich girl, you must get acquainted with one of the right rich girls for you. This usually takes several dates.

On the first date, bring her home early
and don't kiss her good night.

*Conversation is the rich girl's
version of body language.*

THE FIRST DATE

I always consider the first date an educational experience. It's the first appropriate opportunity to explore discreetly the rich girl's interests, values, goals, and private resources. There's no need to ask any questions, since she'll volunteer a great deal of information: she'll want to tell you a lot about herself. Smile a lot, listen intently, and show a genuine interest in everything she has to say. Remember, the more she talks about herself, the more interested she is in you. Conversation is the rich girl's version of body language.

I always suggest doing something very simple on the first date: a movie (only a PG or R rating), a quiet dinner for two (watch what she eats), or a minor cultural event (a play or concert). Never attend opening night, a preview party, or the Night of 1,000 Stars on your first date. Save these for a serious courtship with the right rich girl.

The Perfect Date

Bring her home early and don't kiss her good night. A seemingly indifferent boy can be quite a challenge for the right rich girl. Most rich girls have had everything they want in life and want everything they can't have. Pretend she can't have you (at least at first).

The Second Date

Of course, she accepted. After all, you were a very good listener and she has so many more stories to tell. She can't quite figure out whether you're interested. You were so quiet that she thinks *you're* the mystery.

The second date is your date . . . it's really your very own chance to shine. I expect you to keep control of the conversation, ask a number of polite questions, and volunteer information about yourself. Let her know that you're poor—she'll find it fascinating. Most of my dates could never believe it.

Discreetly display your Prospects: show your sense of humor, exhibit your generosity (tip well), order champagne, share your dessert, and dance if you can. Take her home later than the first date. Kiss her once good night and leave.

The Third Date

Now you know she's interested; she accepted before you even asked.

The third date is designed to impress the rich girl. Continue to signal your Prospects and discuss your vision of the future, your values, goals, and expectations. Leave her with the distinct impression that you're an overachiever, that you can learn to swim, and that you want to contribute.

Take her home late at night, express a tentative sign of sexual interest, then kiss her good night twice and leave.

THE FOURTH DATE

Wait one week. Then invite her to your dormitory, house, apartment, or condominium for an intimate dinner for two. If you can't cook, have the meal catered. Serve champagne *and* Château Margaux. Be gracious and seductive. Wait, however, for a discreet sign of encouragement; I'm sure it will come. (Soon you'll be penetrating the mystery.)

The Perfect Date

Courting the rich girl will require many other dates, including late-night expeditions with her swim to fashionable new restaurants or discotheques, enchanting evenings alone drinking champagne and reading catalogues, or leisurely afternoons at the country club meeting friends of Mummy and Daddy on the tennis courts or the golf course. You will spend intimate evenings alone discussing seating for the next benefit, the sales at Bergdorf's, I. Magnin, or Neiman's, Mummy's new decorator, and Daddy's new philanthropy, or you may simply watch reruns of "Dynasty" or "The Colbys." It will be a romantic interlude you will always remember.

You will, of course, want to take the right rich girl on many perfect dates. The Perfect Date is essential to courting the right rich girl. These evenings, occasions, and outings are especially designed to entertain the rich girl, her Mummy and Daddy, and her swim. You'll want to complete as many Perfect Dates as practically and financially possible, for the Perfect Date is just as important as Your Prospects, the Chain of Giving, and Sex with the Rich Girl. Together they signal to the right rich girl your ultimate intention: a marriage proposal.

Outlined below are five of the many perfect dates. I recommend that you go on as many as possible.

The Perfect Date

OPENING NIGHT

You'll soon learn that rich girls love to open presents (see Chapter 15, "Presents: The Chain of Giving"). They also enjoy attending opening nights. These evenings are the official openings of the symphony, ballet, or opera season and are terribly important occasions. In many large cities, opening night actually marks the commencement of the winter or spring social season. Be sure to mark them on your calendar.

Historically, seats for opening nights at the great opera houses of Europe were reserved for royalty, their noble cousins, and a few rich families. Although we do have a long democratic tradition, opening night could never be considered an egalitarian affair. Instead, it remains a night reserved for rich girls, their Mummies and Daddies, and members of their swim or tribe. It's the rich girl's version of the season opener at Yankee Stadium or Wrigley Field.

Opening night at the opera is a glamorous occasion. It's a tremendous opportunity to display your best friends (diamonds and other jewelry), wear your mink, use Mummy's car and driver, and drink champagne from plastic glasses. Of course, the opera is performed in German, Italian, or French, so it's often impossible to understand; that makes it even more interesting.

I try and attend opening night every year; I hope you'll do the same.

THE EMBASSY PARTY

Rich girls will travel great lengths to attend an embassy party. Ambassadors live in embassies (or a nearby residence), and it's there that they entertain other ambassadors, government officials, rich Mummies and Daddies, and their daughters. I've invited many rich girls to embassy parties and suggest that you take the right rich girl to at least one.

The Poor Boy's Guide

The embassy party is the ideal locale to eat with your fingers (everything is served on silver platters by butlers and maids), drink magnums of champagne, converse in French, and discuss foreign affairs. Unlike opening nights, embassy parties are designed for poor boys: they are free.

The Auction

Old Master paintings in gilded frames, French commodes used by Louis XVI, Georgian silver, and jewelry worn by the Vanderbilts, Goulds, and Liz Taylor are sold at auctions. These "sales" attract rich Mummies and Daddies from throughout the world. Some social critics consider the auction to be the newest version of theater; many *are* held at night and tickets are required. I strongly suggest that you get tickets and invite the right rich girl.

You purchase a catalogue with photographs and estimates of every item (called "lots"), register with a sales assistant (usually a rich girl or society boy), and sit with dozens, and sometimes hundreds, of rich Mummies and Daddies, their advisers, dealers, and other collectors. Auctions are a unique opportunity to see very rich Mummies and Daddies express themselves. The bidding can be frenetic, and the lots can move very quickly. Of course, auctions are particularly fascinating because there's no limit to what you can spend for any one piece. You literally can pay whatever you want. I've seen some Mummies and Daddies get carried away and spend millions for a landscape by Van Gogh, a blue and white piece of porcelain, or a diamond pendant worn by a dead princess. It's an inspiring experience.

The Dinner Party

You already know that rich girls love to eat. Of course, it's never fun to eat alone. It's always much more fun to eat with someone else, and even more fun with several of your friends. A rich girl

The Perfect Date

goes to dinner parties constantly. It's there that her swim meets over radicchio, veal, lobster thermidor, and asparagus tips to discuss trips to Palm Beach, her career, Mummy's walker, and her new catalogues. Whether it's a casual evening or a formal seated dinner, I've always found dinner parties particularly satisfying.

Although the dinner party isn't always food for thought, you and the right rich girl will never go hungry. It's another perfect date and shows your interest in food.

THE COSTUME PARTY

Rich girls love to pretend they are someone else. The costume party is the very best opportunity for her to pretend that she's Scarlett O'Hara, Cinderella, a princess, or a famous French mistress

---

Other Perfect Dates

There are, of course, many perfect dates which suggest the poor boy's imagination, confirm his Prospects, and indicate his varied interests. Each perfect date suggests how well you'll swim or be a member of a tribe. The following list suggests a number of other perfect dates. It's not designed to be exhaustive. Please use your imagination and let your intimate knowledge of the right rich girl guide you.

- The Charity Ball (especially for the rich girl's favorite disease)
- The Polo Game (especially with a picnic)
- The Preview Party (see the play or collection before her less affluent peers)
- The Birthday Party (it must be a surprise)
- The Horse Show (check the circuits for the one nearest you)
- A Day at the Races (sailing or horses)
- Ballooning (especially with Malcolm Forbes)

---

to the King. The perfect costume party requires imagination, old clothes, and a sense of drama—all of which the rich girl has. I suggest that you dress as someone rich or famous . . . an Arab sheik, a well-known explorer, or a dead monarch are all acceptable poses.

My mailbox is constantly stuffed with invitations to costume parties, all arranged by rich girls or society boys. I've never found costume parties to be a drag.

Chapter Fifteen

Presents: The Chain of Giving

A major element, if not the most essential requirement, of courting the right rich girl is the present. Presents are an indispensable feature of the rich girl's life, and without them she ultimately can't survive. For the rich girl, a life without presents is simply no life at all. Historically, many great objects were designed as presents for rich girls (i.e., the Taj Mahal, the Hope Diamond, the clipper ship *Sea Cloud*). Of course, the rich girl has been receiving presents since birth. Mummy and Daddy, her swim, and countless society boys have showered her with boxes and bouquets. She continues to expect them periodically. The rich girl relishes the opportunity of opening any package, however small. Remember, wrap them well, for a well-wrapped present adds to the anticipation and excitement and almost guarantees a successful opening.

The rich girl is terribly appreciative of a gift when it is received and will almost never return it. You must, however, always volunteer to give her the sales slip. This is a necessary display of self-confidence in your own judgment and taste while discreetly admitting that the size may not be right. Always enclose a card with a brief expression of affection. Sign your name.

I have outlined below the appropriate chronological order for providing presents and gifts to the right rich girl. It is critical that you follow this sequence precisely and consistently when dating the rich girl, for each gift has a distinctly different message. The Chain of Giving is the most elemental communication between the poor boy and rich girl, for it establishes your feelings, your level of interest, and your final intention. It is an integral element of courtship and must be followed exactly and precisely. *Never, never break the Chain.*

Months 1–3: Flowers

Begin with daisies or tulips during the first few weeks of courtship and after a month of dating send a bouquet of long-stemmed roses. During months two and three you should send a wider variety of flowers with greater frequency. Include forget-me-nots. Forget-me-nots have a subtle message all their own. Flowers should be sent every few weeks—even if it is just one. Always send cut flowers; plants are for the garden, and Mummy's gardener selects, purchases, and plants these. Furthermore, flowers are meant to die—and, of course, to be replaced.

Months 4–6: Clothing

Never send anything too personal. My friends have always welcomed a Hermes scarf, leather gloves, or even a polo shirt (no imitations, please). A cashmere sweater, although expensive, can be a fitting present for a special rich girl. Never, never give a nightshirt, pajamas, underwear, or any other gift which can be worn at night or in or near a bed. Such gifts are appropriate only after years of marriage.

The Poor Boy's Gift List

$\mathcal{V}$ALENTINE'S $\mathcal{D}$AY

Send flowers, preferably roses, and one box of expensive European candy, preferably crèmes and not solids.

$\mathcal{B}$IRTHDAY $\mathcal{P}$RESENTS

I recommend one nice present. I always suggest moving one step further on The Chain of Giving—e.g., if you're still on flowers, give clothing, if you're on clothing, give jewelry.

$\mathcal{C}$HRISTMAS

You must give her lots of small presents. Her Christmas tree should be littered with gifts from you. I suggest a maximum of ten presents and a minimum of five.

Here's a perfect Christmas gift list for the right rich girl.
- One jar of caviar (make sure it's Beluga)
- One box of Godiva chocolates (an assortment)
- One Hermes scarf (the bigger the better)
- One picture frame (preferably silver from Tiffany, with your picture inside)
- One datebook (with her initials embossed on the front)
- One piece of china
- One book by or about another rich girl
- One major present (something cashmere?)

The Poor Boy's Guide

MONTHS 7–9: JEWELRY

One of my favorite rich friends refers to her jewelry as trinkets. Well, the rich girl loves trinkets of every kind, especially earrings, pendants, brooches, necklaces, pins, and bracelets. These can be a serious and expensive gift, so purchase wisely. I suggest a maximum of one gift monthly during this final period of courtship. Never buy a ring. Poor boys only buy *one* ring, THE RING (see Chapter 18, "Engaged").

MONTH 10 AND BEYOND: FLOWERS AGAIN

Now send only roses; make sure that they're long-stemmed and send lots of them, frequently. Alternate between red and white roses, but never mix the colors. Never send pink roses. This is the final stage of the Chain of Giving.

Of course, other occasions naturally demand a present, the three most important of which are the right rich girl's birthday, Valentine's Day, and Christmas.

Chapter Sixteen

Sex and the Rich Girl

*T*his, unfortunately, will be a short chapter. Sex is incidental to courting the rich girl. Although she certainly enjoys sex, she will make her final judgment about you based on other factors, especially on how you get along with Mummy and Daddy and her friends, the other rich girls, and the society boys which comprise her swim. Most important, she will judge you on your Prospects and your presents. The rich girl is, above all, a realist; she knows the power of sex wanes. Presents (unless they're flowers) can last forever.

Sex, nevertheless, is a key factor which reflects the poor boy's physical and emotional state. Several rules must be observed.

1. **Never have sex on the first, second, or third date.** The poor boy should usually wait until the rich girl provides a discreet sign of encouragement and/or desire. She will do this obliquely and in a roundabout fashion. Favorite signs of encouragement include:
   "I've got to get out of this dress."
   (The silk taffeta dress—after the Palm Beach Ball.)
   "I'm wet."

(In the master suite on Daddy's yawl—the captain is at the helm.)

"I'm too tired to go home."

(After any major charity event.)

"Let's build a fire."

(At Daddy's ski lodge in Vail.)

"Let me show you my room."

(On the estate at Woodside—Mummy and Daddy are in San Francisco for the evening.)

"Riding makes me hot."

(After a trot, canter, or gallop in Middleburg.)

"I just couldn't."

(Anytime—day or night.)

2. **Never joke about sex.** Sex is terribly serious, and Mummy and Daddy never joke about sex. Daddy, as the Great Protector, has completely avoided all discussions regarding sex.

3. **Kiss a great deal.** Rich girls are brought up to kiss everyone: old friends, other rich girls, society boys, and the staff, among others. Rich girls even kiss their horses and dogs. Kissing, in fact, is saying hello, to the rich girl. Kissing the poor boy is an extension of this welcome and should be encouraged at all times.

4. **Never discuss birth control.** All rich girls have their own gynecologist or private doctor; they will have discussed this subject with him. Until you and your right rich girl are married, this is simply not your business.

5. **Pretend that you have had limited sexual experience.** You are neither a novice nor an expert. Mummy has constantly advised her little rich girl to avoid the ladies' man—you must never assume that role. Any poor boy with either too much "experience," "appetite," or "drive" is viewed suspiciously. This diminishes your Prospects.

6. **Never admit that you've slept with a man.** This eliminates your Prospects completely.

7. **Never criticize society boys.** The rich girl has many friends who are society boys. She will probably have uncles, cousins, and maybe even a brother who is a society boy. *You* are never to become a society boy.

8. **Never use your imagination when having sex with the rich girl.** Imaginative sex can lead to kinky sex. If possible think of something else while having sex: Daddy's yacht, the trust funds, the art collection, or the cottage in the Fertile Crescent.

9. **Never, never ask for *that*.**

10. **Rich girls prefer traditional positions.** I suggest that you begin with kissing, petting, and positions named after clergy that seek converts in Africa. Some rich girls do, however, insist on life *and* sex on the top. With the right rich girl this can be a breathtaking experience.

Part Four

❧

The Proposal
and
Engagement

Chapter Seventeen

The Proposal

$\mathscr{Y}$ou've now finished the first three parts of *The Guide* and are convinced that it's the best investment that you have ever made. You're right. Your initial intimidation has gradually disappeared, and you now feel quite comfortable with that very exclusive world of the rich girl. In fact, you've decided that you belong there and are about to make a major decision.

You've come to know a very special rich girl and her family very, very well. You've become very attached to Mummy and have probably spent many hours with her in the kennels and stables. She says that you'll just love Saratoga, and you can't wait until August. (With some luck, you'll soon be breeding on your own.) Mummy's already introduced you to a number of prominent Seniors and her Hot Walker, and you look forward to meeting the entire tribe. You may be receiving late-night phone calls from Mummy's decorator, asking for your advice on the new wallpaper, the *faux* marble mantelpiece, and the suite of Regency furniture he's discovered. Remember, you're not the first poor boy he's called at midnight.

The Poor Boy's Guide

Daddy is pleased. His little rich girl has done well. He encourages you to use his sloop and has had long conversations with you about depreciation and depletion. He compares you favorably to society boys; he starts calling you "son." He's already given you a private tour of the art collection and asks what your favorite painting is—he's most impressed with your knowledge of Old Masters, and Rembrandt in particular. You've made a friend.

The social swim has expanded: you're now part of it. In fact, you're constantly being invited to swim elsewhere. A flood of invitations to benefits, receptions, charity balls, and weddings has developed. You're overwhelmed. The mailman is complaining, and you can't possibly reply to all of them. You've even thought of hiring a social secretary yourself.

In short, you've met the right rich girl and have had a romantic courtship, one which every poor boy should experience. Absolutely everything seems to be fitting into place. You've conscientiously observed all the rules concerning sex with the rich girl and have never broken the Chain of Giving. You've gone on many perfect dates and can still balance your checkbook. You're a very lucky fellow.

It all sounds so hard to believe, but yes, it's true: you've met the right rich girl for you. You're ready, ready for THE **PROPOSAL.**

One cautionary word of advice: Never propose "too soon." The Chain of Giving is designed to last at least nine months and should if at all possible include at least one pre-engagement birthday and Christmas present. The poor boy who proposes too soon does so at his own risk.

My own experience suggests that the poor boy who proposes within a short period of meeting the right rich girl is typically viewed with some suspicion. Justifiably so, he may just be a *prowler.*

A prowler is a poor boy who's determined to break into society at any cost. He may not even have a romantic interest in rich girls, although he's certainly dedicated to making a vertical social ascent with her help. Prowlers wait for broken engagements, personal tragedies (i.e., no date for next week's benefit or charity ball), or simply a lonely and vulnerable rich girl (I know it's difficult to imagine) on whom to pounce. You are never to become a prowler; after all, your motives and intentions can only be described as honorable.

The Proposal

No, I'm not going to tell you where, when, or how to propose. You've come a long way in the last year, and I'm convinced that you'll exercise good judgment in every respect. You're self-confident, in the swim, have good Prospects and, of course, the quiet but crucial support of Mummy and Daddy. I do, however, suggest the following:

1. **Never, *never* elope.** Mummy and Daddy have been waiting years to give their little rich girl a large wedding. Don't ruin it for them (or yourself).
2. **Make sure that you've completed the Chain of Giving.** Don't propose "too soon." Remember, you're not a prowler, you've been invited to swim everywhere.
3. **Propose outside.** Pick a romantic spot—a quiet and secluded corner on Mummy and Daddy's estate or compound is often just right.
4. **If possible, propose during the evening hours.** The rich girl is nocturnal by nature; I've always found her much more agreeable to my own requests at night.
5. **Your proposal should be well conceived and well delivered.** A little nervousness on your part is natural—but too much is not a good thing. Practice beforehand.
6. **Above all, be confident.** You've had a romantic courtship, and

Have a chilled bottle of champagne nearby.

she expects a proposal. In fact she can't wait to set a date. You're about to make her a very happy rich girl . . . after all, meeting you has been the major event in her life.

7. **Have a chilled bottle of champagne nearby.** I suggest Dom Pérignon, which is confidently effervescent and perfect for the Proposal. If possible, drink it out of a glass, not out of plastic cups.

8. **Tell her you need an answer that night.** Don't let her consider too long. When she agrees, propose a toast to your happiness together.

9. **Don't give her a ring that night.** Most rich girls want to pick their own wedding and engagement ring; you may be fortunate and not have to buy a ring at all. (See Chapter 18, "Engaged.")

I've heard incredible tales from many friends about how some poor boys have proposed. I'm told that one poor boy proposed under the White House portico (with the Secret Service and Mummy and the President waiting in the East and West wings). One friend tells me that his college roommate proposed to a Lone Star heiress in a mounted position (he was riding on the family ranch in Kingsville). This poor boy now has a "brand" of his own and hundreds of hired hands. My favorite story is of the poor boy who proposed while sipping the family's very own champagne on a visit to Mummy and Daddy's vineyard in France. This over-achiever claims that Dom Pérignon is *his* patron saint. Of course, he does have a blessed life: he now has planes, yachts, and seats on the stock exchange.

Chapter Eighteen
Engaged

*C*ongratulations, you're engaged. I'm as excited as you, and can't help but think how lucky you are! You're not going to marry just any rich girl; you've found the right rich girl for you. Not too long ago you purchased *The Guide* with, well . . . big hopes. It's simply amazing how one's life can change so quickly and dramatically. You've not only found the rich girl of your choice, you've proposed and she's accepted. Life is truly a marvelous gift, isn't it?

The next few months are going to be very hectic. Mummy and your bride-to-be will be devoting endless hours to compiling the guest list and reviewing designs for the wedding gown, the bridesmaids' dresses, and the wedding trousseau. Your bride-to-be will spend days being measured, draped, and fitted in Belgian lace and silk organza. There will be a marathon of meetings with caterers, florists, engravers, and photographers, and dozens of showers for Mummy and the bride-to-be to attend. It will be an exhausting experience. All this because she's marrying you, a poor boy. It's inspiring. You've suddenly become an example for others to emulate.

Engaged

Although most of the planning and arrangements will be completed by your bride-to-be and Mummy, you're an integral part of this process. I firmly believe that the poor boy should play an active, not a passive, role in planning his wedding to the right rich girl. At the very least you'll be expected to help make many important decisions and attend many social events during your engagement. Before you do anything else, however, you must ask Daddy.

Asking Daddy

My close friends who've married rich girls have all asked Daddy. It's more than an old-fashioned gesture; it's a courtesy which all rich girls' Daddies deserve. Remember, if you've been reading *The Guide* carefully and have been following my advice, he shouldn't be at all surprised.

Asking Daddy is a courtesy which all rich girls' fathers deserve.

The Poor Boy's Guide

You've been spending many weekends with Mummy and Daddy on the estate, compound, or cottage in the Fertile Crescent, and they've been following your progress carefully. Daddy has thoroughly enjoyed your long conversations on the inequities of the tax system and the merits of collecting art. He values your opinions. Your sense of humor, modesty, quiet admiration for Daddy, and willingness to volunteer have all been noticed. He's already convinced that you'll make a perfect son-in-law.

Remember, Daddy may have been a poor boy too. Be confident and courteous and tell Daddy you want to protect and help provide for his little rich girl. (Emphasize "help"; you don't want to do it alone.) I'm sure that Daddy will enthusiastically shake your hand (he may even embrace you) and effusively welcome you into the family. You may be overwhelmed at first, but yes, this is all happening to you. At a later date he'll probably want to devote some time alone with you to discuss your future and that of his little girl. He may even ask what you'd like as a wedding present. I've heard of gracious offers such as a cottage on the family compound, polo ponies, or a down payment on a duplex or triplex. Don't be shy. You may be reluctant at first to accept his offer, but *never turn down a helping hand . . . especially from Daddy*.

Informing Your Parents

Call home and tell Mom and Dad the good news. They'll be overwhelmed and terribly proud: they've raised an achiever. You've given them the peace of mind that only the parents of a poor boy marrying the right rich girl can ever attain. You've made them very, very happy.

Have a long, long conversation with Mom and Dad for, unfortunately, once you've married the right rich girl, you'll be seeing less and less of them. Your social and financial obligations will inevitably keep you miles away.

Engaged

During the period between your engagement and marriage there will be a number of important decisions and responsibilities which you must share with your bride-to-be. You will soon discover that sharing the wealth of the rich girl's life is full of responsibility: marrying the rich girl is a full-time job. For the present time, however, you have the following decisions to consider.

PLANNING THE WEDDING DATE

Don't procrastinate. I'm convinced that an engagement period of four to six months is long enough. Make it shorter if you possibly can. You don't want anything to alter your plans . . . you've simply waited too long and worked too hard for this all to happen. Never, never have "second thoughts"; instead, charge full steam ahead.

WHAT TYPE OF WEDDING

You and your bride-to-be must decide whether your wedding will be a simple (albeit unforgettable) event, or an elegant, formal, and memorable occasion for all the invited to enjoy. Fortunately, most rich girls have formal weddings, and in general, the formality of the wedding influences the size of the guest list.

Mummy and Daddy have waited many years for this event, and they will certainly have hundreds of guests to invite. Your bride-to-be will probably want a large wedding as well; she'll need to invite everyone from her swim, former classmates from prep school, and summer friends from the Fertile Crescent. She'll probably also choose a large wedding party . . . a dozen or more bridesmaids and an equal number of ushers.

Personally, I prefer a large formal wedding. Your marriage is a significant social event and you should plan it accordingly. After having attended scores of weddings, I'm persuaded that poor boys look their best in Oxford gray cutaways with striped trousers, gray waistcoats, and striped ascots surrounded by hundreds of elegantly attired guests. I hope you'll agree.

The Poor Boy's Guide

*T*HE *A*NNOUNCEMENT

Although Mummy and the bride-to-be will make sure that the appropriate newspapers and magazines are advised of the engagement, you may have a few special publications (alumni magazines, *USA Today,* and *The New York Times*) in which you want the engagement announcement to appear. This is an important event, so please publicize it.

If Mummy and Daddy are major public figures, heirs to large fortunes, or subscribers to *Town & Country,* they may want to invite the press to both the engagement party and wedding ceremony. I would encourage this as well.

*T*HE *B*RIDAL *R*EGISTRY

This is where the fun really begins. Major department and specialty stores offer a free service which allows you and your bride-to-be to list almost all the items you will ever need for your life together. Each gift purchased is recorded so that no one using the registry will duplicate a selection. Remember, the larger the wedding, the longer the guest list, and the greater number of gifts you must register for (and will receive). You will register for fine bone china, sterling silver, crystal stemware, punch bowls, Georgian decanters, champagne coolers, and elegant candelabras. The choices to make are endless. It's just like being on a game show, but you're already the winner.

You can, of course, register at a number of different stores and locations, for registering is really a courtesy for your guests—it saves them a great deal of time and effort. One of my closest friends (he married a Lone Star heiress) spent several days registering at stores throughout the country, including Tiffany & Co., Neiman-Marcus, and I. Magnin. He called this a North American registry. His wedding attracted guests (and comment) throughout the world.

Engaged

The bridal registry:
this is where the fun really begins.

Selecting the Rings

Your bride-to-be and you will select the engagement and wedding rings together. Since diamonds are among her best friends, expect her to be very knowledgeable. She'll know precisely what she wants. Do everything to please her, although this may be a very expensive purchase so budget your money accordingly. You may have to pay yet another and (I hope, final) visit to your local banker.

You may, however, be lucky. Mummy or Mummy's Mummy may want her to have a family ring, called an heirloom. Don't object—it's a tradition many rich girls follow. I'm all for traditions.

The Poor Boy's Guide

The Marriage Contract

Some Mummies and Daddies, no matter how enthusiastic they are about the upcoming marriage, may request that you sign a marriage contract. Some people are just cautious by nature. Mummy and Daddy may have a contract themselves, and they may want to protect their little rich girl's assets, dividend income, or royalties from the oil and gas wells. If such a request is made, don't object. Instead, welcome the opportunity to discuss the family finances. Consult your own lawyer and negotiate in good faith. Remember, *all* contracts can be renegotiated at a later date.

The Guest List

Mummy will ask you to submit a list of guests whom you would like to invite. Although you may be limited to a few hundred or more, there certainly will be room for most of your close friends. Please be considerate and try and remember all those individuals who've helped you along the way. (You may write to me, care of the publisher.)

I strongly suggest that you invite any columnist, social secretary, or society boy who has given you a helping hand. Be generous and invite a few poor boys who haven't been as lucky as you. Remember, marrying the right rich girl is a social obligation which all poor boys should undertake; you are improving society, and your example should encourage others to do the same.

The Ushers

I'm advised by a well-known wedding consultant that the socially accepted ratio is one usher per fifty guests. For small weddings, this will mean a dozen or more ushers; for larger weddings up to twenty. Your brothers, your bride-to-be's brother(s), members of the swim, and society boys are excellent choices for ushers. Society boys make the very best ushers . . . they are excellent walkers.

Engaged

THE BEST MAN

Choose your father, brother, or your very best friend. Never choose a society boy, although they make perfect ushers; having a society boy as the best man may raise more than one eyebrow.

THE BACHELOR PARTY

I'm sure that your close personal friends, a number of admiring poor boys, and members of your swim will want to give you a bachelor party. We've all been to bachelor parties, and they can be great fun. Just keep level-headed and please don't get carried away. You don't want any troublesome stories appearing in the columns or rumors circulating among the wedding party.

THE REHEARSAL DINNER

Traditionally, you (or your family) will be expected to organize and pay for this evening prior to the wedding day. You'll be judged by the success of the rehearsal dinner, so please don't spare any effort or money. Ask for Mummy's advice on planning this evening. She'll be able to offer valuable suggestions on an appropriate venue, menu, and music.

Members of the wedding party, the bride-to-be's family, your family, and all out-of-town guests should be invited. This is a preview of your wedding, so order as much champagne, caviar, and *foie gras* as you can possibly afford. You want everyone to leave thinking how fortunate the bride-to-be is to have met you.

Of course, you'll be toasted many times, so be exceptionally gracious and polite. I suggest ending the evening with a toast to Mummy and Daddy, thanking them for making this all possible.

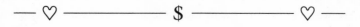

The rehearsal dinner was quite a success. Get a good night's rest. The last few months have been hectic, but you're on the first step to a truly elevating experience. It will be a lifelong experience that few boys will ever enjoy.

Your Share

Traditionally, the groom has fewer wedding responsibilities than the bride-to-be; he also has fewer expenses. There are, however, a number of costs which even the poorest boy must be prepared to bear. It's the final installment in your investment in the future.

Your Bride-to-Be's Engagement Ring
The Wedding Rings
The Bride's Flowers
A Wedding Gift for the Bride
Gifts for the Best Man and Ushers
The Rehearsal Dinner
The Clergy's Fee
The Honeymoon

I'm really quite impressed with the magnitude of your success. You were among the many millions of poor boys languishing at society's doorstep, never quite willing to knock at its door. You escaped this tragic social lethargy by embracing a goal and a very special girl. You not only knocked on society's door, you opened it to find a new and wonderful life and the right rich girl. I never thought that you would succeed so easily and so naturally—even *I* could learn from your experience.

Think of what you may want to do next. You're achievement-oriented, so you'll want to set new goals each and every year. You may want to be an ambassador, sail for the America's Cup, or simply retire to Lexington and breed. I've had friends who have pursued a life of endless contribution: they support all the diseases, run for higher office, or head charitable foundations and trusts. You have so many more options now that you've found the right rich girl; you're an inspiration to each and every remaining poor boy.

Marrying a rich girl is the best revenge.

Appendices

Appendix A
The Poor Boy's Dictionary

The rich girl has developed her own distinctive vocabulary. It's a lexicon which constantly betrays her special circumstances and exclusive world. It's much, much more than a dialect and should be considered a language in its own right. If the poor American boy is to communicate successfully with the rich girl of his choice, he must, of course, first understand her. It is the author's hope that the following glossary of terms will benefit each and every poor boy and will preclude any unneccessary confusion.

Beluga (n): Not a whale, silly; one of the finest forms of caviar and the rich girl's favorite snack.

C.B. (n): Abbreviation for confirmed bachelor. A gentleman over thirty, whom no one expects to marry.

Car (n): Limousine; a rich girl never refers to a limousine as a "limo"; it is simply a "car."

Chukker (n): A period of play in the game of polo.

Circulate (v): One of the principal reasons that rich girls work: to meet as many rich girls and society boys as possible.

Climber (n): An individual obsessed with society and determined to join a swim or tribe at almost any cost (see **Prowler**). Avoid any association with climbers.

Coming out (n): Nothing to do with gays and closets; this is one of the rich girl's most important evenings, her debut or presentation to society. Daddy and Mummy normally pay a small fortune for this evening. Go if invited.

Committee (n): A group of rich girls and society boys who plan benefits for charity together.

Contribute (v): Another employment objective of the rich girl; the act of giving one's time and money to and for the benefit of society.

Cottage (n): A summer residence of twenty-five rooms or more; historically associated with Newport, Rhode Island, this term is now used with a wider geographic reference.

Coupon (n): A dividend or interest payment that supplements the rich girl's income from work, Mummy, and Daddy.

Daddy (n): A rich girl's father.

Daily (n): Help which works during the day; the opposite of live-in.

Dark Harbor (n): Not a soap opera or a movie starring Bette Davis; the most subdued but most exclusive resort in the Fertile Crescent.

Darling (v): Pronounced "daahling"; translates as "hello," an expression usually accompanied by a kiss on the cheek. Seniors use this greeting constantly; Juniors less so.

Deb (n): A rich girl who has come out. Abbreviation for "debutante."

Driver (n): Chauffeur; the rich girl typically has a car and driver, usually Mummy's, when she needs one.

The Poor Boy's Dictionary

Duplex (n): an apartment, condominium, or co-op with two floors; two-thirds of a triplex.

Escort (n): A younger society boy, rich boy, or poor boy who accompanies a rich girl throughout the evening of her debut.

Fertile Crescent, The (n): The geographic area which extends from Point O'Woods, Fire Island, to Northeast Harbor, Maine. The summer playground of many rich girls and the source of the rich girl's civilization.

Fishers (n): An island in Long Island Sound between Connecticut and New York, part of the Fertile Crescent. Most of this island is private, as in "no entry." The guards are friendly but insistent. Home of the old rich.

Gossip (n): The traditional form of conversation between two rich girls or a rich girl and a society boy.

Hard hat (n): Nothing to do with the construction trade or union workers who whistle at poor girls on the street; headgear worn when riding a horse, usually black or brown with an elastic strap to keep it on. A must-purchase by every poor boy with a serious interest in horses.

Heiress (n): A very, very rich girl who has an established, sizable, and well-publicized inheritance; the perfect rich girl for an overachiever.

Help (n): Anyone who works for the rich girl or her family, including a maid, butler, driver, gardener, or live-in.

Hot-to-trot (adj): A rich girl who is ready and willing to have sex with a poor boy.

Hot Walker (n): An older society boy (usually a C.B.) who is a constant escort for a rich girl's Mummy. The most valuable and useful part of a Walker is his elbow; alternatively, an individual who walks a polo pony between chukkers.

The Poor Boy's Guide

Junior (n): A younger member of a country club, social club, or benefit committee, usually between the ages of twenty-one and forty. Juniors have reduced fees and contributions, and attend special functions designed for their age group.

Live-in (n): Help which lives with the rich girl's family in separate quarters.

Lockjaw (n): The social disease of the rich girl and her family. Originated in Locust Valley, Long Island. Nonfatal, but highly contagious.

Magnum (n): Not a gun; the traditional name of the bottle for the rich girl's favorite tonic, champagne.

Mousse (n): Not an animal found in Maine; one of the rich girl's favorite desserts, usually chocolate or vanilla, and usually yours.

Mummy (n): A rich girl's mother.

Nanny (n): A rich girl's nursemaid and *ex-officio* member of the rich girl's family.

Networking (n or v): One of the poor boy's major goals . . . establishing as many contacts with rich girls and their friends as possible. Meet one rich girl and you can meet them all.

Noblesse oblige (n): Contemporary theory that it is the social obligation of the poor boy to marry a rich girl.

Overachiever (n): A poor boy who marries a very, very rich girl (see Appendix C: "The Honor Roll").

Philanthropist (n): A rich girl's Daddy who gives at least part of his money away.

Pictures (n): Not the movies; paintings, usually by French Impressionists or the Old Masters.

Pinkie (n): Definitely not a communist sympathizer or a finger on the hand; formal riding attire traditionally worn during a fox hunt.

Polo (n): Not a designer label, but a game which originated in Afghanistan, played with horses, mallets, and eight players. A favorite pastime of the rich girl's brother and father.

Premarital (adj): A word used to describe sex before marriage (see Chapter 16, "Sex and the Rich Girl").

Prenuptial (adj): A term used to describe an agreement establishing a specified property settlement before marriage to a rich girl. You may be asked to sign this. Consult your lawyer.

Prep (v): To go away to private school before college.

Prowler (n): An individual who is constantly trying to break into high society.

Scandal (n): Anything newsworthy which happens in Palm Beach.

School (n): College or prep school.

Season (n): The period of time during the calendar year when many benefits or charity events are held. Alternatively, the season in Palm Beach from late December through early March.

Senior (n): A member of a country club, social club, or benefit committee above the age of forty. Members of tribes are Seniors; Juniors join swims.

Shelter magazines (n): The term used to describe those magazines which publicize and advertise a rich girl's home life— i.e., *House & Garden* and *Architectural Digest*.

Social Register (n): A book found in most rich girls' homes; sometimes called the green book or blue book (its real color is black), it lists the rich girl's family, relatives, and friends together with their schools, clubs, and occupations. Recommended reading for every poor boy.

Society boy (n): A young man (i.e., a Junior) who devotes the majority of his time to organizing and attending benefits, charity balls, dinner parties, and other social events. He is dedicated to Society and is the constant companion of the rich girl and her very best friend.

String (n): Nothing to do with a cloth or rope; a group of polo ponies, usually five or more.

Summer (v): To spend the summer with other rich girls and society boys, usually in the Fertile Crescent or some other exclusive resort.

Swell (n): A member of a tribe or swim with exceptional social graces; a welcome addition to any party.

Swim (n): Absolutely nothing to do with the butterfly or crawl; the social circle which a rich girl joins after college. You are either in the swim or not, and jumping in the neighbor's pool won't help.

T & C (n): Slang for *Town & Country* magazine.

Terribly (adv): Very; e.g., *terribly* expensive.

Transatlantic (n): A rich girl who spends a significant amount of time on both sides of the Atlantic; she may live in the United States, but she shops in London, Paris, and Milan.

Tribe (n): A group of rich and influential Seniors, both male and female, who socialize together. Tribes are the rich Seniors' version of a swim.

Trot (n): The gait of a horse between a run and a walk, in which the legs of a horse move in diagonal pairs. Faster than a walk, slower than a canter.

Trust (n): A monetary fund set aside for a rich girl for future use. A trust sometimes provides current income in the form of dividends or interest.

Vineyard (n): Absolutely nothing to do with wine; Martha's Vineyard, an island off Cape Cod and within the Fertile Crescent. Increasingly popular with rich girls.

Vital Statistics (n): Those private assets of a rich girl which truly distinguish her: her trust funds, dividends, royalties, and inheritance.

Walk (v): To escort a very social Senior; some Seniors teach poor boys to walk.

Wheeler (n): An elderly (i.e., Senior) Hot Walker.

Appendix B
Recommended Reading

$\mathcal{T}$he serious reader will want to broaden his knowledge of the rich girl, for *The Guide* is designed to serve as an introduction and not a *catalogue d'raison*. Each reader, in fact, may have a particular interest which he wants to pursue in greater depth. I certainly encourage independent research of every conceivable kind.

I have collected an extensive library of the literature of the rich girl, which I have found to be of great assistance and which I depend on constantly. I recommend that every poor boy attempt the same. The books and periodicals summarized below should provide an excellent start for just such a collection.

$\mathcal{F}$ICTION:

An American Tragedy
by Theodore Dreiser
1925, Horace Liveright, Inc.

The story of Clyde Griffiths, a poor boy who meets and falls in love with the rich and beautiful Sondra Finchley. Unfortunately,

he is forced to murder his poor (and pregnant) girlfriend Roberta
Alden. An American classic and precisely the situation the poor
boy must avoid. Clyde's punishment is death by electrocution.
Required reading for all poor boys.

The Rich Are Different
by Susan Howatch
1977, Simon and Schuster

Although set in the period from 1922 to 1940, this book admirably conveys the world of the rich girl and society boy. The
lessons here are eternal and all poor boys will benefit from reading
this extravagant novel. There's a message in the title which recalls
Scott Fitzgerald's and Ernest Hemingway's most famous conversation: they both agreed that rich girls were different than their
less affluent peers.

The Great Gatsby
by F. Scott Fitzgerald
1925, Charles Scribner's Sons

I read Fitzgerald's great classic annually. Jay Gatsby had the right
idea; he simply picked the wrong rich girl. Daisy, by the way,
was wrong, for rich girls *do* marry poor boys. Another sad story.
I suspect Jay would have profited from reading *The Guide*. He'd
probably be alive today.

I Came as a Thief
by Louis Auchincloss
1972, Houghton Mifflin

Certainly not my motto, for I want to share the wealth, not steal
it. I do, however, enjoy the title. This is the story of a poor Irish
boy who marries the only daughter of an old and prominent New
York family. One of the many novels by Auchincloss that explore
the very special world of the old rich. I've read them all.

An American Dream
by Norman Mailer
1965, The Dial Press

What a nightmare. This novel spans thirty-two hours in the life of Stephen Richards Rojack (a poor boy), who married the immensely wealthy Deborah Caughlin Mangaravidi Kelly, a descendant of English bankers, Bourbons, and Hapsburgs. Unfortunately, Stephen didn't pick the right rich girl: their relationship is sheer murder. Young Norman at his very best.

NONFICTION:

The Rich and the Super-Rich: A Study in the Power of Money
by Ferdinand Lundberg
1968, Lyle Stuart

A very thick book (over 800 pages), full of facts and figures, on the rich and how they make and spend their money. Although published more than fifteen years ago, this book remains the leading survey of the extent and concentration of American wealth. Lundberg lists names, lots of them, so this is particularly worthwhile for the poor boy with a good memory for hard facts and vital statistics.

The Art of Eating
by M. F. K. Fisher
1976, Vintage Books

My favorite book on food. Fisher transcends the world of cookbooks and creates an aura that compels the reader to accept the premise that eating well may be the best revenge. Literate, humorous, and a must addition to any poor boy's library.

Recommended Reading

**The Right People: A Portrait of the
American Social Establishment**
by Stephen Birmingham
1968, Little, Brown

Birmingham has made a profession of writing about the social establishment, and in this book he concludes that high society is alive and well. This volume is full of photographs, anecdotes, gossip, and personal reminiscences about the lives of America's upper class. It's fascinating reading by a writer who knows more about society and its institutions than anyone (Cleveland Amory and the present author excepted) else. Stephen also published **Real Lace** (on the Irish rich) and **Our Crowd** (about the Jewish rich). I recommend all three.

Who Killed Society?
by Cleveland Amory
1960, Harper & Brothers

My favorite testimonial to the world of the old rich. Amory is a master of the anecdote and superb at detailing the aristocratic traditions of families like the Vanderbilts, Astors, Biddles, and Drexels. He answers the question we've all been asking: Who and what killed proper society? His indictment is broad but well delivered. Must reading for the overachiever.

Palm Beach
by John Ney
1966, Little, Brown

Ney writes about Palm Beach as if it were a religious experience. He worships this golden littoral and argues that Palm Beach is the most beautiful thing that American society has created. I think he's right. This small volume is laced with amusing stories, social history, and marvelous photographs of famous rich girls and their Mummies and Daddies. It's an excellent primer for your first visit to Palm Beach.

Charlotte Ford's Book of Modern Manners
by Charlotte Ford
1980, Simon and Schuster

Every poor boy should have at least one book on social expectations, manners, and etiquette. Charlotte is a rich girl herself (she is the daughter of Henry Ford II), and she provides valuable advice for almost every conceivable situation. Whether it's protocol, debutante parties, or marriage contracts, I turn to this volume regularly. Charlotte, of course, writes with the voice of experience.

$\mathcal{B}$ IOGRAPHY:

The Queen: The Life of Elizabeth II
by Elizabeth Longford (Countess Longford)
1983, Alfred A. Knopf

In my opinion, the best biography of a rich girl who takes her career seriously. This book also provides valuable insights into a rich girl's taste in clothes, travel, food, and housing. As an additional incentive, it is the story of a rich girl who married a poor boy. Highly recommended.

Texas Rich
by Harry Hurt III
1981, W. W. Norton

A biography of H. L. Hunt, who made a fortune in oil, and his three (yes, three) families. Hunt had fifteen children, so there are a lot of younger Hunts and former Hunts around. A well-written introduction to oil money and Daddy.

Recommended Reading

Poor Little Rich Girl
by C. David Heyman
1983, Lyle Stuart

A fascinating biography of one of this century's most legendary rich girls. Babs Hutton was the granddaughter of Frank W. Woolworth; her aunt was Marjorie Merriweather Post. She defined the concept of the heiress.

This book moves from Palm Beach and Southampton to the South of France and is full of rich girls, society boys, princes, and princesses. PLRG reviews Babs's marriages to seven ("The Magnificent Seven") poor boys. Whenever I'm feeling a bit depressed, I read this book; it's an immediate pick-up.

Little Gloria . . . Happy at Last
By Barbara Goldsmith
1980, Alfred A. Knopf

Gloria Vanderbilt, who else? My favorite book chronicling the childhood of a rich girl. It's full of insight and packed with names like Morgan, Whitney, Drexel, and Firestone. A good read. Gloria, by the way, is still available.

The Rockefellers: An American Dynasty
by Peter Collier and David Horowitz
1976, Holt, Rinehart and Winston

An important chronicle of America's premier dynasty (forget the Carringtons). The authors brilliantly relate the history of four generations of this unique American institution, beginning with John D. Sr., who amassed an incredible fortune. The story ends with the fourth generation, many of whom appear very willing to share the wealth.

The Poor Boy's Guide

The Social Register
A must purchase; this volume, published annually, lists thousands of rich Mummies and Daddies and their daughters.

Yachting
This magazine is one of the oldest published on Daddy's favorite sport. If you live within fifty miles of a lake, bay, or ocean, I suggest you subscribe as well.

Country Life
Published in England, this magazine is read on both sides of the Atlantic. It's full of stories about the English aristocracy, their country houses, horses, and dogs. Mummy loves to read it on the way home from London.

National Enquirer
Junk, but a good summer read at the beach or on the boat.

Antiques
Probably the most authoritative guide to antiques published in the U.S. Mummy and Daddy use this to shop for furniture. It can also be a very good guide of the shops, galleries, and decorators where the rich girl works or frequents.

Apollo
The premier art magazine. Very serious and global in perspective. A must if Mummy and Daddy collect pictures or are in the art trade.

Palm Springs Life
A chatty journal which provides more than enough information on this desert enclave of the rich. Although the crowd is often a bit old for a Junior, many a rich girl has relatives here.

Recommended Reading

The Celebrity Register
This volume is published periodically (about every ten years) and provides complete biographical information on many rich Mummies and Daddies.

Town & Country
Probably the most widely read periodical among the rich. Excellent photography and educational features on rich girls throughout the country. You simply must read *T & C* for a full appreciation of her world. I receive two copies monthly in case I lose one.

Vanity Fair
Tina Brown has done wonders with this magazine. What a comeback for Condé Nast. Although it's not dedicated to the rich girl, this magazine certainly applauds her lifestyle.

W
An extraordinary publication. More pictures per subscription dollar than any other magazine. My friends prefer their photographs in this journal over those of any other publication. It's always a thrill to pick up a copy and see all your friends at the latest benefit or fashion show. Very international in scope, so it is recommended for the frequent traveler.

In my preface to *The Guide,* I argued that the most productive and dynamic societies were characterized by the frequency at which poor boys marry rich girls. I further suggested that it was the social obligation, the *noblesse oblige,* of the poor boy to marry a rich girl. It's an obligation which I hope you will all accept and endure.

Poor boys have, of course, been marrying rich girls for centuries. There are a very few men, however, who merit special mention because of their impressive accomplishments in this field. They have been notable practitioners of *noblesse oblige* and sharing the wealth. They are the overachievers who have married very, very rich girls.

In their memory I have created an Honor Roll, lest we forget that these boys will never die poor.

H.R.H. Prince Philip, Duke of Edinburgh.

Born June 10, 1921, on the Greek island of Corfu. Educated at private schools and the Royal Naval College, Dartmouth. Married

The Honor Roll

Her Royal Highness, the Princess Elizabeth, now Her Majesty, Queen Elizabeth II of Great Britain.

Philip married one of the wealthiest and most powerful women in the world. The Queen's fortune was recently estimated by the British press to exceed three billion dollars. She has a palace in London, several castles (Windsor, Balmoral), and a house (Sandringham). She's the owner of a priceless art collection, magnificent jewels, and many stallions. Philip, by the way, was a poor Greek boy and is still lovingly called "Phil the Greek" by many adoring subjects. Philip is the classic "overachiever."

Present Occupation: Prince
Issue: Charles, Anne, Andrew, Edward
Interests: Wildlife, carriages, polo
Address: c/o Buckingham Palace
                                       Buckingham Palace Road
                                       London SW1, England

Charles Spittal Robb.

Born Phoenix, Arizona, June 26, 1939. Graduated from the University of Wisconsin (B.B.A.) and the University of Virginia (J.D.). Married Lynda Bird Johnson, the President's daughter, on December 9, 1967, in an elaborate ceremony at the White House.

Chuck, who received a bronze star, also merits a position of distinction on the Roll. As a social aide to the White House (a form of protocol), Chuck met Lynda Bird . . . it was love at first sight. Lynda's mother, Lady Bird, amassed a sizable fortune in real estate and communications properties while her husband pursued a successful political career. Chuck has followed in his Daddy-in-law's path and was a very popular governor of Virginia. Although a Democrat, Chuck is one of the earliest practitioners of *noblesse oblige;* he's enjoyed sharing the wealth of a rich girl's life.

The Poor Boy's Guide

Present Occupation: Presidential Candidate
Issue: Lucinda, Catherine, Jennifer
Interests: Politics
Address: Hunton & Williams
3050 Chain Bridge Road
Fairfax, Virginia   22030

Claus Von Bulow.

Born Claus Cecil Borberg in Copenhagen in 1926. Changed name to "Bulow" in early 1940s and added "Von" when he moved to New York. Educated at private schools in Switzerland and Cambridge University, where he graduated with a degree in law in 1946. Married Martha "Sunny" Crawford von Auersperg at a small family ceremony in the chapel of New York's Brick Presbyterian Church.

Claus married the only child of utilities magnate George Crawford, who accumulated a fortune in the natural-gas business in the early 1900s. Sunny's inheritance has been estimated to exceed seventy-five million dollars. The Von Bulows shared a wonderful life together as well as a vast apartment on Fifth Avenue and a cottage in Newport, Clarendon Court. This twenty-room mansion on Bellevue Avenue was built in 1904 and modeled after a Palladian manor house. The 1956 movie classic *High Society,* with Grace Kelly, Bing Crosby, and Frank Sinatra, was filmed here. The Von Bulows had a fairy-tale existence.

Present Occupation: Socialite
Issue: Cosima
Interests: Leather
Address: 960 Fifth Avenue
New York, New York   10021

The Honor Roll

Stephen E. Smith.

Born September 24, 1927, in Bayport, Long Island. Graduated from Georgetown University in 1948 with a B.A. in Social Sciences. Married Jean Kennedy at New York's St. Patrick's Cathedral in May 1956.

Jean Kennedy is the youngest daughter of Rose and Joseph Kennedy, Sr., and the sister of Joe Jr., Jack, Bobby, and Teddy. After briefly working for a family concern (his family's), Stephen joined the Park Agency Inc. (the Kennedy family holding company), which manages and controls various Kennedy family trusts, properties, and investments, including the fabled Merchandise Mart in Chicago. He has been called the minister of finance of the Kennedy clan. Reliable estimates of the Kennedy family fortune range from $350 million and up. Jean's share is considerable.

Present Occupation:	Manager of family fortune
Issue:	William, Stephen Jr., Kym (adopted), Amanda (adopted)
Interests:	Kennedy campaigns, his children
Address:	Park Agency Inc.
	125 Park Avenue
	New York, New York 10016

Bernard Shaw.

This former policeman and divorced father of three married Patricia "Patty" Campbell Hearst on April 1, 1979, two months following her release from prison. Patty had received a Presidential commutation of her bank robbery sentence, after serving twenty-two months of a seven-year sentence. Patty was kidnapped by the Symbionese Liberation Army in February 1974, and was the object of a nationwide manhunt.

Bernard married the daughter of Catherine Campbell Hearst

and Randolph Hearst, the Chairman of the Board of the Hearst Corporation, a privately owned chain of newspapers, magazines *(Town & Country)*, television and radio stations, with interests in ranching, timber, real estate, and paper manufacturing. Her grandfather was the illustrious press lord credited with inventing tabloid journalism. Bernard met Patty while moonlighting as a bodyguard when she was free on $1.5 million in bail in 1977.

Present Occupation:	Chief of Security, Hearst Corporation, New York
Issue:	Gillian
Interests:	His family, weight lifting
Address:	c/o The Hearst Corporation 959 Eighth Avenue New York, New York 10019

Rafael Lopez Sanchez.

This Argentinian writer married Paloma Sphynx Picasso, the daughter of Pablo Picasso, in May 1978 at the town hall on the Left Bank of Paris. She wore a red, black, and white toreador-style outfit designed by friend Yves Saint Laurent. The occasion was magnificent, more like a bullfight than a wedding. Rafael wore a white suit and a white matador's hat. It was a terribly festive occasion.

Rafael married an heiress to the greatest collection of twentieth-century art, one that was said to total 1,995 paintings, 2,000 drawings, 1,226 sculptures, and thousands of ceramics and lithographs. Although the estate was divided among other siblings and a significant donation to the French government was made, Paloma's share was valued in the millions. Paloma is an artist in her own right and her jewelry is worn by other rich girls and their

Mummies throughout the world. Although quiet by nature, Rafael is well known for his humor.

Present Occupation:	Playwright
Issue:	None
Interests:	Fashion, philosophy
Address:	c/o Tiffany & Co.
	727 Fifth Avenue
	New York, New York 10021

Appendix D

The Poor Boy's One Hundred

Certainly, one of the easiest ways to identify a rich girl is through her name. In the United States there are a number of families, or extended families, whose names are synonymous with wealth. They may be descendants of the robber barons (Harriman), the first true American industrialists (Ford, Du Pont), the publishing empires (Hearst, Pulitzer), or the merchant families that traded money (Morgan) or grain (Cargill). There are, of course, recent additions where invention (Land) or ingenuity (Packard), or where a natural resource (typically oil) has generated a fortune (Getty, Hunt). Many of these families have had their money for generations and can properly be considered dynasties.

There are even families whose incomes have been based on beer and alcohol (Coors, Busch, Bronfman, Stroh, and Kennedy).

Although these are some of the names to remember, the list is not designed to be all-inclusive. The serious reader will want to undertake his own research.

The Poor Boy's One Hundred

Allen (Investors)
Bancroft (Publishing)
Bechtel (Construction)
Belk (Merchandising)
Bronfman (Distillers)
Burden (Chemicals)
Busch (Beer)
Cabot (God)
Chandler (Publishing)
Clark (Sewing Machine)
Coors (Beer)
Cox (Communications)
Crow (Real Estate)
Cullen (Oil)
Danforth (Food)
Davis (Oil/Entertainment)
Dayton (Merchandising)
Deere (Farm Equipment)
Dillon (Banking)
Disney (Entertainment)
Donnelley (Printing)
Doubleday (Publishing)
Du Pont (Explosives/
   Chemicals)
Fairchild (Cameras)
Field (Merchandising/
   Investments)
Firestone (Tires)
Fisher (Automobiles)
Forbes (Publishing)
Ford (Automobiles)
Fribourg (Grain Trade)
Galvin (Electronics)
Getty (Oil/Trusts)
Gimbel (Merchandising)

Grace (Chemicals)
Haas (Blue Jeans)
Hass (Chemicals)
Harkness (Oil)
Havemeyer (Sugar)
Hearst (Publishing)
Hewlett (Electronics)
Hillman (Steel)
Hilton (Hotels)
Hope (Entertainment)
Houghtons (Glass)
Hunt (Oil/Real Estate)
Johnson (Wax/Personal Care
   Products)
Kaiser (Steel)
Kennedy (Investment)
Kennedy (Liquor)
Kleberg/Johnson (Ranching)
Land (Cameras)
Laughlin (Steel)
MacMillan (Grain)
Marriott (Hotels/Food)
McCabe (Paper)
McCormick (Farm Equip-
   ment)
McGraw (Publishing)
Mellon (Banking/Investments)
Morgan (Banking)
Mossbacher (Oil)
Newhouse (Publishing)
O'Connor (Ranching)
Olin (Chemicals)
Ordway (Manufacturing)
Packard (Electronics)
Paley (Broadcasting)

The Poor Boy's Guide

Perot (Electronics)
Phipps (Steel)
Pillsbury (Food)
Pitcairn (Glass)
Pritzker (Finance)
Pulitzer (Publishing)
Reed (Timber)
Reynolds (Metals)
Reynolds (Tobacco)
Richardson (Pharmaceuticals)
Robins (Pharmaceuticals)
Rockefeller (Oil/Real Estate)
Rosensteil (Distillers)
Rosenwald (Merchand./ Invest.)
Schlumberger (Oil Service)
Scripps (Publishing)
Searle (Pharmaceuticals)
Smith (Banking)
Staley (Food)
Stephens (Investment Banking)
Strauss (Merchandising)
Stroh (Brewing)
Sulzberger (Publishing)
Temple (Timber)
Tisch (Hotels/Tobacco)
Upjohn (Drugs)
Walton (Merchandising)
Wang (Wang)
Watson (I.B.M.)
Weyerhaeuser (Timber)
Whitney (Investments)
Wrigley (Chewing Gum)

Author's Note

Regrettably, I haven't found the right rich girl yet, although I've come close on many, many occasions. I have, in fact, always been extraordinarily difficult to please: I wanted to go to Palm Beach on my very first vacation (age four); I only got as far as Atlantic City. I am convinced, however, that I will soon be successful in finding the right rich girl . . . for in my heart, I know that I'm an overachiever. In *your* heart you know whether you're a poor boy or not; I certainly don't have to tell you. I've always considered myself *the* authentic poor boy, since I realized at a very early age that I would someday have to support myself. Sure, it was a shock at first, but I've gradually come to accept it . . . at least temporarily. For a long time, I thought I was the *only* poor boy. It's such a relief to know that there are others.

The Guide, of course, was designed to assist poor boys . . . but once you've met and married the right rich girl, you may consider giving it to another poor boy, or even a rich boy or society boy. I'm hopeful that everyone, even the rich girl, can benefit from reading *The Guide.*

Notes
and
Clippings

Notes and Clippings

Notes and Clippings

Notes and Clippings